KU-572-157

YOU ALWAYS CHANGE THE LOVE OF YOUR LIFE

(FOR ANOTHER LOVE OR ANOTHER LIFE)

AMALIA ANDRADE

First published in Spanish as Uno siempre cambia al amor de su vida (por otro amor o por otra vida) by Espasa, an imprint of Editorial Planeta Colombiana S.A., Bogotá, Colombia

Published in the United States in 2018 by Penguin Books
An imprint of Penguin Random House LLC, 375 Hudson Street, New York, NY 10014

This edition published in Great Britain in 2019 by Orion Spring
an imprint of The Orion Publishing Group Ltd
Carmelite House, 50 Victoria Embankment
London EC4Y 0DZ

An Hachette UK Company

10 9 8 7 6 5 4 3 2 1

A CIP catalogue record for this book is available from the British Library.

ISBN (Hardback) 978 1 4091 8096 8
ISBN (eBook) 978 1 4091 8097 5

www.orionbooks.co.uk

Set in Questa Grande

Designed by Amalia Andrade Arango and Sabrina Bowers

Printed in Italy

FOR LA MAMMA,
WHO TAUGHT ME THAT LOVE
IS A SUPERPOWER

FOR MOM

ONE THING I AM NEVER GOING TO DO WHEN I GROW UP
Is fall in love, drop out of college, learn to subsist on water and air, have a species named after me, and ruin my life.

— NICOLE KRAUSS,
The History of Love

Is there a word for when you are young and pretending to have lived and loved a thousand lives? Is there a German word for that? . . . Let's say it's Schaufenfrieglasploit.

– AMY POEHLER,
Yes Please

BEFORE YOU START READING

This book is for (oops!) you if you are heartbroken because:

☐ The love of your life is gone.

☐ You let the love of your life go and now you are regretting it (deeply).

☐ You were born with a broken heart.

☐ You are heartbroken over the death of your dog, cat, or boa constrictor.

☐ You broke up with your best friend.

☐ You broke your own heart.

☐ Someone you love very much has passed away.

☐ You broke up with your imaginary boyfriend / girlfriend.

☐ OTHER: ______________________

____

____

(Write your emotional situation here, total anonymity guaranteed.)*

* NOT APPLICABLE TO BEYONCÉ, TINA FEY, BRADLEY COOPER, OR RYAN GOSLING.

ALTERNATE TITLES

1. What People Promise When They Are in Love: How to Deal with Broken Promises, Broken Hearts, and Other Related Complications

2. Heartbreak: A Portable Encyclopedia of Bad Romances, Bad Breakups, Bad Vibes, and Other Related Feelings

3. ____________________

(Write your own title here.)

TREAT YOURSELF TO STICKERS

stickers (available wherever stickers are sold) can be used whenever you feel you are making progress. Any sparkly star sticker, smiley face sticker, good job sticker, or the kind of stickers that smell good if you scratch them (not you, licorice sticker, you suck) will work PERFECTLY FINE for the purposes of this book. Use a sticker when:

- You haven't cried in public in over a week.
- You have refrained from writing passive-aggressive tweets and/or Instagram captions.

- you haven't asked your friend who follows him/her on Instagram to show you pictures in more than three days.

- You have showered, gone to work, and eaten a proper meal in the past twenty-four hours.

CHAPTER

CRY

ONE

ING

The act of producing tears, often while making loud sounds due to pain, sorrow, joy, or need. Usually accompanied by wails and sobs.

I've never told anyone, but I carry with me an unresolved love. A silent, private love that no longer exists and that no one even knows existed. A love I never put to an end; a love that hasn't even ended. There are times when I want to cry over her, but I can't. I've tried to cry over anything and everything else: a movie, a song, my mother's own grief, that YouTube video where a man proposes to his sweetheart while a band is playing a Bruno Mars song, a picture of a dead cat.

But I can't. I can't cry.

I can't cry over her and I know it's not a good sign. Those tears are going to end up accumulating in some secret part of my body, maybe my elbow or pinky toe. Maybe, one day, when I slam my elbow against a door or bang my toe against the foot of the bed, I'll cry like I've never cried before: I'll throw myself on the ground and I will—at long last—cry for her as I lie there, unable to get up for an hour, two hours, five hours, or more.

Sometimes I think that if I never cry for her, I won't forget her, I won't wash her name from my body. And sometimes (most of the time, actually) I don't want that to happen. I want her to stay here with me, forever a pain in my elbow.

A LIST OF THINGS THAT DEFINITELY DO NOT WORK RIGHT NOW

- Sending text messages that are longer than a handwritten letter and contain the words "I hate you," "I hope you die an awful death," and/or "You are the worst thing that ever happened to me." *

* THIS APPLIES TO EX-BOYFRIENDS, EX-GIRLFRIENDS, AND BEST FRIENDS. DOES NOT APPLY IF YOUR CAT RAN AWAY OR YOUR DOG DIED.

- sending text messages that are longer than a handwritten letter asking for forgiveness for having sent the previous message.

- sending naked selfies (please don't do this).

- Using witchcraft or any kind of sorcery to get your loved one back.

- compulsively stalking your loved one via Instagram, Twitter, Facebook, Snapchat, etc.

- Deleting your loved one from all your social networks in a flash of hatred ~~and~~ only to add him/her again five minutes later.

- Watching any romantic movie (especially *Blue Is the Warmest Color*, *When Harry Met Sally*, *Beginners*, or *Eternal Sunshine of the Spotless Mind*).

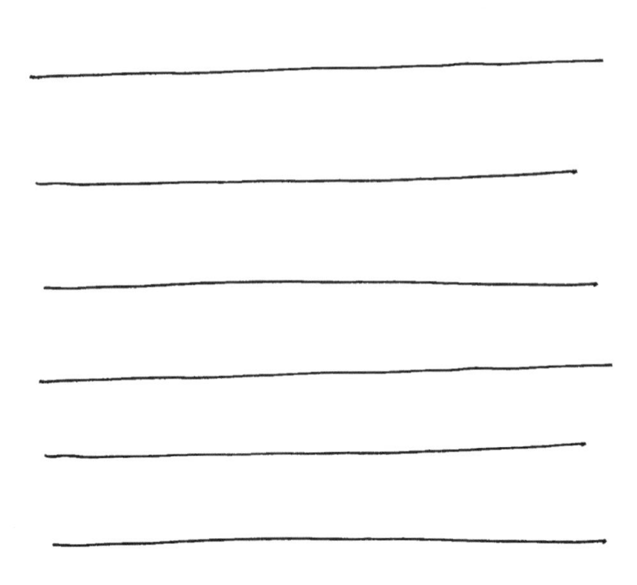

(Write your own list of things you wish were working right now but, sadly, are not.)

A LIST OF THINGS THAT ABSOLUTELY DO WORK RIGHT NOW

EXAMPLE: ____________________

____

(I am not yet aware of anything that works at this stage. If you do happen to know of anything, please share the wisdom. Tear out this page and mail it to Penguin Books, 1745 Broadway, New York, NY 10019 or email it to:

thiswillsaveyourbrokenheart@amaliaandrade.com

While we wait for someone to invent a pill that makes you forget selected memories, or for Lacuna Inc. to open their world headquarters, I suggest you do the following:

- Indulge yourself to a certain extent. For example: Eating ice cream and crying with friends = GOOD. Eating ice cream and crying while stalking your ex = NOT GOOD.

- Find distraction in social gatherings. You'll still feel miserable inside, but your mind will be occupied with things other than your pain.

- Really allow yourself to inhabit your sadness. I recommend you always keep your sunglasses handy, buy waterproof mascara (if you wear mascara), and say things like: "I'M NOT CRYING, I JUST HAVE A GARBAGE TRUCK STUCK IN MY EYE."

- Follow a basic diet consisting of pizza, cereal, chocolate, salads, and tuna (see page 209 for recipes specifically catering to each stage).
- As my tía María Eugenia used to say: "There's no sadness that milk and cookies can't cure."*
- Sing "Un-break My Heart" by Toni Braxton, "Hello" by Adele, or "All By Myself" by Céline Dion while you cry in the shower.
- Cry, cry, and cry some more. Tears have invisible superpowers that will help you heal.

* TÍA MARÍA EUGENIA NEVER ACTUALLY SAID THIS BUT IT'S THE KIND OF THING SHE WOULD TOTALLY SAY.

(Write a list of things that do work for you and NEVER forget them.)

INFALLIBLE MECHANISM FOR OVERCOMING SADNESS

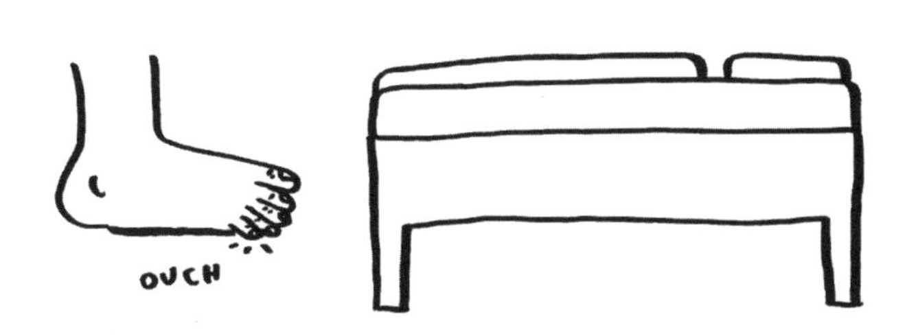

BANGING YOUR PINKY TOE ON THE FOOT OF THE BED

TUMBLR
PORN

MASTERS OF EMOTIONS

SELENA GOMEZ

High Priestess of Toxic Love

"I KEPT IT ALL TOGETHER TO WHERE I WOULD NEVER LET YOU DOWN, BUT I KEPT IT TOO MUCH TOGETHER TO WHERE I LET MYSELF DOWN."

ROLAND BARTHES

Pontifex Maximus of Love Discourse

"LANGUAGE IS A SKIN: I RUB MY LANGUAGE AGAINST THE OTHER. IT IS AS IF I HAD WORDS INSTEAD OF FINGERS, OR FINGERS AT THE TIP OF MY WORDS."

RENÉE ZELLWEGER

MEG RYAN

JENNIFER ANISTON

Holy Trinity of the Romantic Comedy

"YOU LOOK LIKE A NORMAL PERSON BUT ACTUALLY YOU ARE THE ANGEL OF DEATH." — When Harry Met Sally

LENA DUNHAM

Deacon of Chronic Pessimism

"NOT THAT KIND OF GIRL."

SHAKIRA

Mother Superior of BAD Romantic Decisions

BEYONCÉ

High Priestess of All Things Love

"I'VE BEEN THROUGH HELL AND BACK, AND I'M GRATEFUL FOR EVERY SCAR."

VOGUE - SEPTEMBER ISSUE - 2018

ORSON WELLES

Bishop of Emotional Assertiveness

"WE'RE BORN ALONE, WE LIVE ALONE, WE DIE ALONE."

PEOPLE WHO'VE HAD IT WORSE

INSTRUCTIONS: Tear out or xerox (is that really a verb?) this page and keep it in your wallet or any other place where you will have easy access to it. Use it whenever you think nothing will ever be good again (or before you cry in front of your boss/friends for the eighth time in a week).

- Hillary Clinton after the 2016 elections.
- The president of Malaysian Airlines.
- The Kardashian brother (yes, the Kardashians have a brother).

- Michelle, no one's favorite member of Destiny's Child. (Sorry, Michelle. But just because you aren't our favorite doesn't mean we don't love you.)
- Kylie Jenner's lips.
- Florentino Ariza from *Love in the Time of Cholera* by Gabriel García Márquez.*
- Dante because of Beatrice.
- Selena Gomez because of Justin Bieber, and vice versa.
- Monica Lewinsky.

* IF YOU HAVEN'T READ THIS BOOK, GO BUY IT, NOW. NOT ONLY IS IT PERFECT, IT WILL ALSO GIVE YOU A RENEWED FAITH IN LOVE (AND TRUST ME, YOU NEED LOTS OF THAT FAITH RIGHT NOW).

MONICA LEWINSKY

MEDICAL EXPLANATIONS

1. DEFINITION OF HEARTBREAK

noun | heart·break | /ˈhärt-ˌbrāk/

- A very strong feeling of sadness, disappointment, etc.
- Crushing grief, anguish, or distress.

— Merriam-Webster

This definition is way too concise in my opinion. I don't think it encapsulates the drama and torment of the matter. They should seriously consider redefining the word, and I am willing to take on this very important task, pro bono, because I am that good of a person. I already have a few thoughts on the subject:

Heartbreak: noun | heart · break | /ˈhärt-ˌbrāk/

- Living death.
- The worst thing you could wish upon someone.
- A permanent hole in your stomach, a perpetual desire to cry.

2. REASONS WHY YOUR HEART FEELS LITERALLY BROKEN

When you break your heart, or when someone else does it for you, your bones ache in places you didn't even know you had bones, and your chest hurts in a way that could be described as a "fake heart attack."

Physical pain and emotional pain both activate the same regions of the brain: the somatosensory cortex and the posterior insula.

That's why emotional pain LITERALLY hurts.

There's also a condition known as broken-heart syndrome in which, when a person suffers a strong emotional impact or loss, the heart shows all the signs and symptoms of a heart attack, though with completely different medical ramifications. In other words, it's a "non-heart-attack heart attack." NOT GOOD.

3. INSOMNIA

Insomnia is one of the most common side effects of heartbreak, and it is, quite honestly, a curse. Being heartbroken is like having the flu: during the day, you can get by (more or less) but as soon as the sun goes down, you want to die. Insomnia can be produced by such things as:

- Fear of dreaming about things related to your loss.
- High levels of cortisol.
- compulsive thoughts and trying to control them.

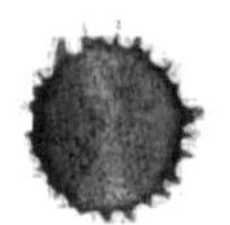

THIS IS WHAT HAPPENS WHEN YOU DECIDE TO WRITE A BOOK WITH A FOUNTAIN PEN.

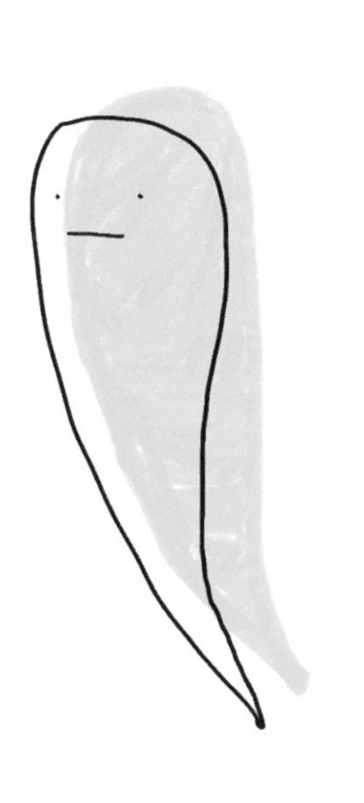

CHAPTER

SELF-
DESTR

TWO

UCTION

The destruction of one's self.

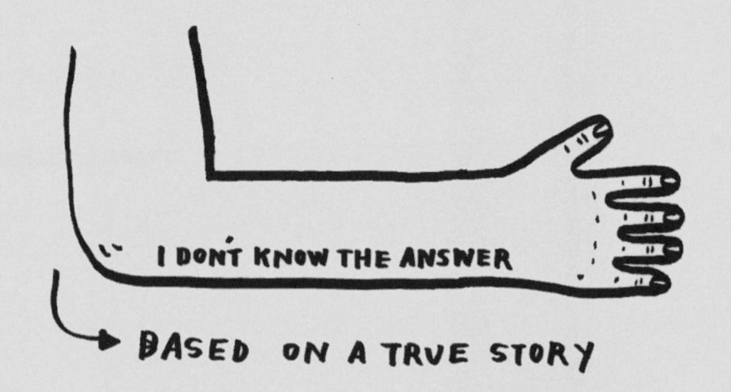
I DON'T KNOW THE ANSWER
BASED ON A TRUE STORY

I don't know how many times I've tried to write about her, and I just can't. Words pile up on top of each other, but they can't survive outside of me. I don't want to name her because to love is to name, and what I feel for her now isn't the opposite of love, but it isn't anywhere close to love either. It's a foreign emotion. Anger and gratitude.

I can't write her name without feeling my hand burn. I can't think of her body without feeling regret. I wish this wasn't the case. I wish I could say that everything happens for a reason, that maybe this story has always been a part of me. But that wouldn't be true. I can't talk about the many ways in which she broke me forever. I can't explain how or why, but after her it was hard for me to understand that love isn't necessarily the same thing as first love. It was hard for me to understand that is, and always will be, what happened to me with her. But that being in love is better.

I hide some of my deepest pains in what I don't write about her: what it feels like when your love can't reach the other person, the part of your body where rejection hurts the most, the taste in your mouth when you see the person you love kissing someone else.

I can't talk about her because talking about her would mean talking about myself.

LOVE ADDICT RECOVERY KIT

SELF-ESTEEM PILLS

(which someone should sell because we are in the twenty-first century, which was supposed to be future but here we are and there are still no flying cars, no self-esteem pills, and most hand dryers STILL fail to dry hands).

EXERCISE (OR AT LEAST TRY TO)

READ THIS BOOK

ADOPT A KITTEN

START BELIEVING IN SOMETHING OR SOMEONE (SUCH AS ELLEN DEGENERES).

EMPOWERING CDs (OR SPOTIFY PLAYLISTS).

MOVIES THAT WILL MAKE YOU LAUGH AND BELIEVE EVERYTHING IS GOING TO BE ALL RIGHT

CHART SHOWING THE LEVEL OF IMPORTANCE GIVEN TO A NUMBER OF DETERMINING FACTORS DURING A BREAKUP

(Based on real data gathered from a WhatsApp group chat)

IMPORTANCE YOU PLACE ON YOURSELF AND YOUR WELL-BEING.

YOUR DREAMS/GOALS/PERSONAL AND PROFESSIONAL PROJECTS.

YOUR SUPPORT SYSTEM (FRIENDS AND FAMILY).

THE PERSON WHO BROKE YOUR HEART.

WHAT THIS PERSON IS DOING WITH HIS/HER LIFE NOW THAT YOU AREN'T TOGETHER.

TIME SPENT OVERANALYZING/INTERPRETING TWEETS.

NUMBER OF TIMES THAT PERSON LIKES OTHER PEOPLE'S PICS ON INSTAGRAM.

FIGURE 2. Real-Life Scenario

IMPORTANCE YOU PLACE ON YOURSELF AND YOUR WELL-BEING.

YOUR DREAMS/GOALS/PERSONAL AND PROFESSIONAL PROJECTS.

YOUR SUPPORT SYSTEM (FRIENDS AND FAMILY).

THE PERSON WHO BROKE YOUR HEART.

WHAT THIS PERSON IS DOING WITH HIS/HER LIFE NOW THAT YOU AREN'T TOGETHER.

TIME SPENT OVERANALYZING/INTERPRETING TWEETS.

NUMBER OF TIMES THAT PERSON LIKES OTHER PEOPLE'S PICS ON INSTAGRAM.

SELF-DESTRUCTIVE BEHAVIOR CHECKLIST

After A LOT of crying comes self-destruction. I wish I could say that this phase goes away as you become more mature, but I'm afraid that's not true. When you were a teenager, this meant drinking Mike's Hard Lemonade (or whatever alcoholic beverage mixes liquor with fruit juice and is sold at the corner store), but now that you're an adult it means turning off your cellphone, spending an entire day in bed, and handing work assignments in late because "I haven't been able to concentrate," which actually means:

"I've spent a week binge-watching a Netflix series and I don't feel like doing anything else."

Below you will find a checklist of self-destructive behaviors that are commonly undertaken by anyone who has a broken heart. This will help you determine where you are on a scale from zero to 2007-shaved-head-Britney-Spears.

From the following list, select the behaviors you identify with:

☐ Falling into the impossible task of finding the first message/phone number on a napkin/email/Instagram comment that the person responsible for breaking your heart ever sent you.

- ☐ Getting a tattoo (usually of an existential phrase such as "I DON'T KNOW THE ANSWER" or "THIS TOO SHALL PASS") that you will regret for the rest of your life. Trust me, I know.

- ☐ Playing "Someone Like You" by Adele on repeat. (If this song doesn't apply to you, please write your favorite depressing song here: __________________________.)

- ☐ Not showering for two days or more.

- ☐ Not keeping the promises you made to yourself.

- ☐ Eating a donut every day at four o'clock for a month (this also applies to chocolate, ice cream, gummy bears, and any other high-calorie food).

- [ ] Shaving your head.
- [ ] Torturing yourself with cheesy ballads from the '90s and '00s by artists like Roxette and/or Ryan Adams. If you are a millennial and you have no idea what I'm talking about, think of an emo power ballad or something like that.
- [ ] Stop working (in order to watch Netflix).
- [ ] Avoiding your friends, hiding from your editor, leaving a group chat (in order to watch Netflix).
- [ ] Watching Netflix until the judgmental question "ARE YOU STILL WATCHING?" appears on the screen. Yes, it's been six hours and I'm still watching because the world stinks and I don't feel like doing anything else. Plus, series today are more addictive than crack. Please let me be.

☐ Not eating (because most foods and/or restaurants remind you of the person who broke your heart).

☐ Virtually or physically stalking the person who broke your heart (though the second option is significantly creepier and borderline criminal).

☐ Losing all sense of pride, going as far as to forget what it even means. Here's the definition, just in case.

PRIDE:

(Come to think of it, maybe you should just write this one yourself.)

YOU MAKE
MY HANDS
SHAKE

RESULTS

Evaluate your behavior/current emotional state based on the number of items you checked on the previous list:

FROM 0–4: NOT BRITNEY AT ALL

you are an emotional intelligence billionaire, which is better than owning a gazillion shares of Apple stock. IT's also possible that you lied. In that case, all I can say is that this isn't a real test and there is absolutely no need to cheat. (Yup, that's me reprimanding you.) There are no shortcuts to getting over a broken heart. THE ONLY WAY OUT IS THROUGH.

On the other hand, it just might be the case that you don't have a broken heart and that you bought this book because:

a. You are my mom. (Hi, Mom! Look, I wrote a book!)

b. You want to support debut authors and illustrators. (If this is the case, THANK YOU. I need it. I quit my job to do this.)

c. By revisiting, however briefly, past events that have made us feel fragile, vulnerable, and broken down, we remember that it is thanks to them that we are now strong and powerful.

FROM 5–9: OOPS! YOU DID IT AGAIN

You fall within the "normal" range of self-destruction, if there even is such a thing. Experts (that is, those of us who are rehabilitated compulsive self-destroyers) recommend that you redirect your feelings toward CONSTRUCTION and not destruction, especially when it comes to yourself. To that end, you can take on one of the following projects:

- Draw a map of your favorite pool when you were a kid and mark the areas where you liked to play, where you memorably bumped your head, where you had your first underwater kiss, where you ______________________

______________________________ (insert memory here).

- Buy a bag of colored pencils and change the names to personality traits you like about yourself.

  EXAMPLE: Blue = Best Blues shower Singer Ever

- Write the email you wish you would receive.

FROM 10-14: BALD BRITNEY

The good news about being where you are is that you will come out of this completely renewed. The bad thing is that you'll have to go through hell to get there, if you aren't in hell already. This might sound odd, but even if it's hard to believe right now, you are in a very fortunate position. The chinese believe that CRISIS also means OPPORTUNITY and therefore having a broken heart offers us the opportunity to die and be born again. Dying and being reborn over and over again, with all the pain this entails, is what life is all about.

Don't forget that the measure of pain is sometimes also the measure of love, and we are capable of loving precisely because we allow ourselves to be vulnerable. There is no better way to navigate this world than with your heart on your sleeve.

P.S: Britney endured what she endured so that we wouldn't have to. Every time you think you can't take it anymore, remember this: IF Britney made it through 2007, you can make it through this day.

ON THE MEANING OF SELF-DESTRUCTION

According to my theory (actually it isn't my theory; it's something I learned from talking to my therapist), there are two schools of thought when it comes to self-destruction.

The first and most obvious one comes from a reductionist perspective: self-destruction ~oops! means hurting oneself in any way, be it physically or emotionally (for example, drugging yourself in order to feel numb or cutting yourself so you can physically feel emotional pain).

The second is the belief that self-destruction is a way of deliberately distancing yourself from yourself.

In other words, turning down the volume on your life. Self-sabotaging your happiness. Kicking your own lunch box. Saying "I know what I'm doing" when actually you have no idea what you're doing other than the fact that what you are doing is entirely wrong. It's sleeping until 2:00 p.m. on a Wednesday. It's working your brains out so you don't have to stop and think. It's hurting yourself on an emotional level, creating toxic relationships with people, places, things, or feelings that make you feel so incredibly bad that you actually feel somewhat good.

TYPES OF INTERNAL MONOLOGUES

(Also known as conversations you have with yourself when you are emotionally broken. These monologues are the shortest road to Self-Destructionland.)

INSTRUCTIONS: SELECT THE MONOLOGUE THAT BEST SUITS YOU.

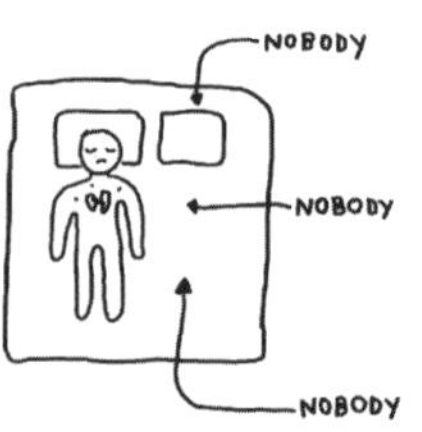

INTERNAL MONOLOGUE No. 1

"I'm never going to get over this."

INTERNAL MONOLOGUE No. 2

"I'm going to be alone for the rest of my life."

INTERNAL MONOLOGUE No. 3

"I'm never going to find anyone like him/her."

INTERNAL MONOLOGUE No. 4

"Love is bullshit."

INTERNAL MONOLOGUE No. 5

"I want to die."*

Add your own INTERNAL MONOLOGUE here:

____

____

____

*DISCLAIMER

If you are having suicidal thoughts or if you have self-harm concerns, there are some things you should know:

1. You are NOT alone.

2. Talk to someone about how you are feeling.

3. Ask for help. (Asking for help is in NO WAY a sign of weakness; on the contrary, it shows that you are BRAVE.)

4. Call the National Suicide Prevention Lifeline: 1-800-237-8255.

THE DEATH-REBIRTH CYCLE

SELF/ESSENCE/THAT INNER VOICE THAT HAS ALWAYS SPOKEN TO YOU:

Life is filled with noise that stops us from hearing this voice and prevents us from reconnecting with ourselves. Being reborn will always mean going back to that voice and making room for the silence you need in order to listen to it.

FALSE SELF/EGO:

It will die more than once and the process is painful. But after pain, there will always be light.

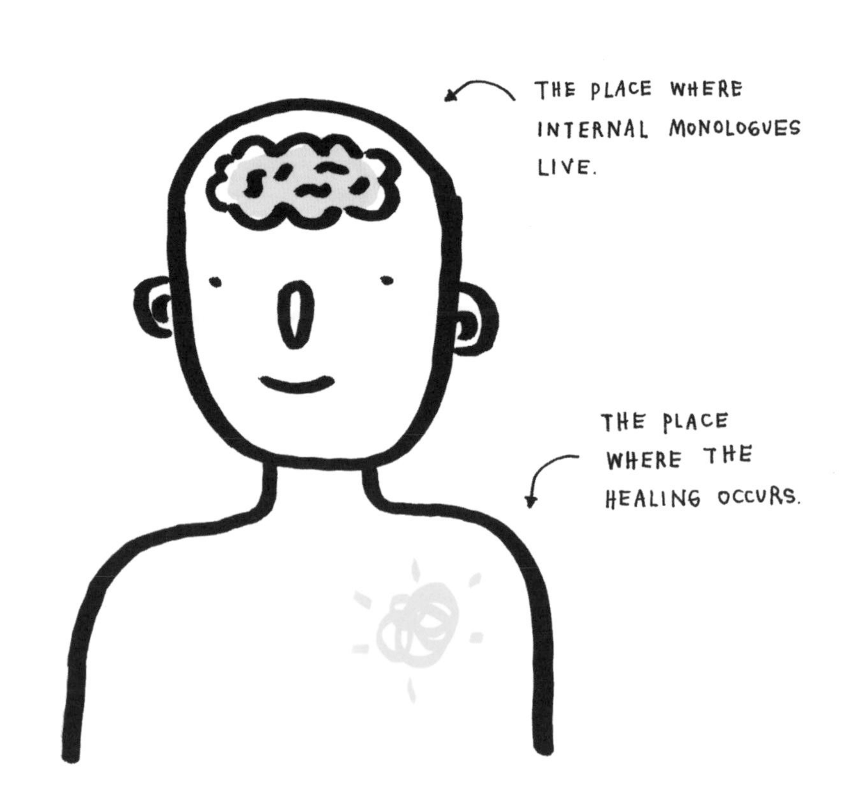
THE PLACE WHERE
INTERNAL MONOLOGUES
LIVE.
THE PLACE
WHERE THE
HEALING OCCURS.

Write down your most creative self-destruction methods. Doing this will help you rationalize your self-destructive feelings and perhaps even help you deconstruct them, making them disappear forever.

NOTE: I tend to be a firm believer in the idea that creativity can take on anything, and it must permeate every aspect of our lives... EXCEPT for this one. In this case, I vote for always being honest with ourselves and not getting too caught up in finding new and creative ways to hurt ourselves. This, according to me (and probably Eckhart Tolle), is one of the secrets of happiness.

IF I HAD YOUR PHONE NUMBER, I WOULD TEXT YOU THIS MESSAGE:

NOTE: THIS WOULD BE A GOOD TIME TO FIND A MENTOR WHO HAS ALREADY BEEN THROUGH SOMETHING LIKE THIS AND CAN HELP YOU. IF YOU CAN'T FIND ONE, YOU CAN COUNT ON ME. THIS MESSAGE IS PROOF OF IT.

CHAPTER

ANGER, REVENGE, OTHER FEEL

THREE

AND RELATED INGS

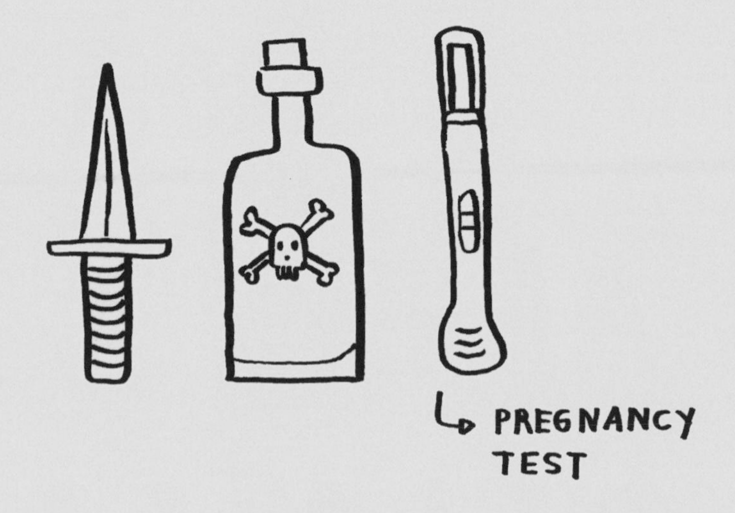
PREGNANCY
TEST

I once had a dream where a woman came up to me, face-to-face, but instead of kissing me, she sucked out all my words right through my mouth. They didn't come from inside me; they were on my skin, and as she sucked, the words all rolled up together, from my feet to my lips, flowing into her and cleaning out everything along the way.

At the end of the dream, I could still speak perfectly fine, but I was never able to say what I really wanted. All I could produce were mistaken versions of my own thoughts.

Stealing someone's words is the best kind of revenge, I thought when I woke up.

HOW TO INSULT SOMEONE WITH SWEET TALK

A CONCISE DICTIONARY OF PASSIVE-AGGRESSIVE TERMINOLOGY

I'm not mad, I'm just disappointed.

MEANING: I'm seriously pissed off and I'm about to kill you.

It's my fault for expecting something from you.

MEANING: It's all your fault.

It's too late now, don't worry about it.

MEANING: I'm never going to forgive you . . . EVER.

(READ 11:45 P.M.)

MEANING: This nonsense doesn't deserve a response.

You just don't think about those things.

MEANING: You don't think.

I hope everything is going well.

MEANING: If everything's going great for you but not for me, I'll kill you.

I hope you don't regret this.

MEANING: I'm on a mission to make you regret this for the rest of your life.

I've already said everything there is to say.

MEANING: Next, I'll explain EVERY mistake you've ever made in your life.

It just doesn't occur to you that I . . .

MEANING: You're the most selfish person I know.

I just can't count on you.

MEANING: If I nag you enough, maybe I can...

NOTES ON ANGER

Love is hard, but it's harder to finish *Super Mario Bros.*, and we all did it when we were kids/teenagers. While you're going through the process of healing a broken heart, a certain amount of anger is considered acceptable and even necessary. Anger is a good thing because it lets us get rid of repressed feelings or unfulfilled emotions that we don't know how to express in any other way. Still, there's a big difference between being passive-aggressive and kidnapping the dog that belongs to the person who broke your heart.

Use one of these bills issued by the Bank of Emotional Intelligence to reward yourself every time you feel like doing something out of anger but don't, when you feel like getting some revenge but hold off, or when you beat back some purely hateful thoughts.

(BILLS AVAILABLE ON FOLLOWING PAGE ⟶)

500
MERYL STREEP
500
~BANK of EMOTIONAL INTELLIGENCE~

300
OPRAH
300
~BANK of EMOTIONAL INTELLIGENCE~

100
SELENA QUINTANILLA
100
~BANK of EMOTIONAL INTELLIGENCE~

THIS FEELING
IS BIGGER
THAN ME.

HOW TO WITHDRAW MONEY FROM YOUR BANK OF EMOTIONAL INTELLIGENCE ACCOUNT

- ☐ Stop reading his/her tweets.
- ☐ Stop driving past his/her house.
- ☐ Realize that you're not the Taylor Swift of *Red*, you are the Taylor Swift of *1989*.
- ☐ Don't ask your friends to show you his/her pics on Instagram.
- ☐ Stop going to places where your ex might be.

- ☐ stop blaming yourself.
- ☐ stop blaming him/her.
- ☐ Avoid filling up his/her inbox with a ton of spiteful emails.
- ☐ Resist the temptation to call his/her mother/boss and tell them your darkest secrets.
- ☐ Avoid liking tweets and Facebook posts more than two years old.

SWEEP AWAY YOUR SORROWS

WHY IT'S NOT A GOOD IDEA TO AND SABOTAGE HIS/ HER

BAD KARMA.

YOU HAVE TO SEE THEM WITH OTHER PEOPLE.

IF YOU PLAY WITH FIRE, YOU'RE GOING TO GET BURNED.

STAY FRIENDS WITH YOUR EX
LIFE FROM THE INSIDE

IF YOU LOANED HIM/
HER CASH, YOU'RE
NOT GETTING IT BACK.*

* The same goes for clothes.

BECAUSE, LIKE MY
MOTHER WOULD SAY,
"THERE'S NO NEED."

CHAPTER

DEPRE

FOUR

SSION

A syndrome characterized by profound sadness and the inhibition of normal psychological function, often accompanied by neurovegetative disorder (whatever that means).

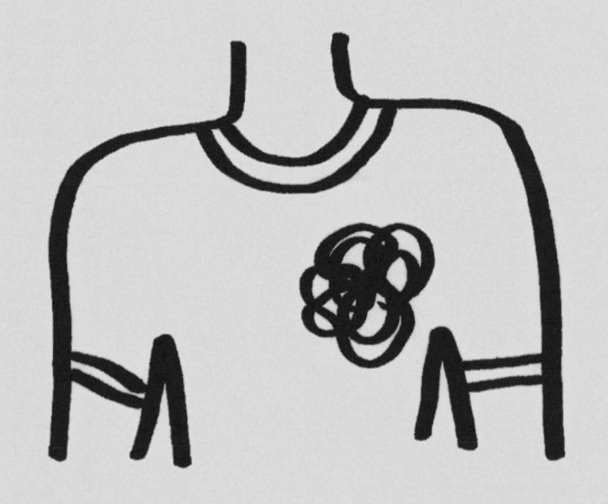

"I didn't realize it"—is what I was told. "Now that you mention it, I can see it all clearly, but I didn't realize it back then."

How was that possible? The signs were all there, like a fog in the air that I had to brush away from my face as I walked from place to place. I had to move them aside like furniture as I walked from the bedroom to the living room and from the living room to the kitchen, and by the time I wanted to go back into some part of that tiny house, they had already crowded together again into a bigger pile than before. They were spreading faster and more out of control than the undergrowth in some crowded and forgotten part of the jungle in some far-off country whose name people are never certain how to pronounce. The air was thick. When I slept (that is, when I could sleep) there was a tightness in my chest. It's asthma, I thought. Or anxiety. It's stress from work. It's the fact that several days have passed since I wrote anything worthy, and when that happens, I start to feel half dead inside.

Now I can remember that Wednesday down to the last detail. The pale yellow sheets that were on the bed, the necklace that belonged to A.'s mother hanging around her neck, the spoon she had used to stir her coffee lying on the floor. It had slipped from her fingers, and she left it there.

Our invisibilities had brought us to that place, the tiny deaths, the succession of tiny little deaths, the things we didn't say to each other, the things we didn't know how to say, the feelings we knew were there but didn't know how to conjure up.

It wasn't a sum of these things. It was the space between them.

It wasn't the things that we lost. It was not realizing that we were losing them.

HOW TO TELL IF YOU ARE DEPRESSED

You know you're depressed when you feel tired all day, when you burst into tears in the middle of the afternoon for no apparent reason, when you can't tell if what you've got is sadness or nausea or both, when you're constantly sick to your stomach, when self-deception no longer works, when the misery sits there day after day, when hope has turned into denial.

You know you are depressed when:

(COMPLETE THIS FORM ~~YOURSELF~~, SO IT ENDS UP BEING SOMETHING WE'VE WRITTEN TOGETHER: OUR LITTLE TREATISE ON IDENTIFYING DEPRESSION.)

DEPRESSION= DESPERATE MEASURES

This is the stage of grief where you feel so overwhelmed that you are willing to accept any sort of help/ intervention as long as it makes you feel a little bit less miserable. But some types of help are better than others. Here is a list of moderately desperate and very desperate measures that you may find yourself considering. My advice: stick with the first set.

1. MODERATELY DESPERATE MEASURES (WILL MAKE YOU LESS MISERABLE)

- Going to Mass with your mom/aunt/grandmother.

- Taking a few drops of Rescue Remedy (which is actually a "flower essence" mixed with A LOT of brandy) and then letting the miracles happen. Listen when I tell you that this is the best thing you can do for yourself right now.

- Going to see a psychologist/psychiatrist. (This isn't desperate, it's actually quite sensible. At least as sensible as taking Rescue Remedy.)

- Going to see a fortune-teller/palm reader/expert in tarotology.

- Going on blind dates set up by your friends.
- Getting a totally new, very regrettable haircut.
- Buying a pair of problematically expensive ass-kicking boots.
- Thinking of leaving the country / permanently changing your name.

ADD OTHER MODERATELY DESPERATE MEASURES HERE:

- ____________________
- ____________________
- ____________________
- ____________________
- ____________________

2. VERY DESPERATE MEASURES (THESE YOU SHOULD DEFINITELY AVOID, AS THEY WILL INEVITABLY MAKE YOU MORE MISERABLE):

- Drinking psychedelic tea.
- Believing that the best way to get over someone is to get under someone else.
- Calling your ex and inviting him/her to a "casual" lunch.
- Trying to be best friends with your ex.
- Trying to be best friends with your ex's best friends.
- Performing an exorcism.
- Getting into witchcraft or other new-agey stuff.

- Having sex with strangers.
- Faking your own kidnapping.

• ADD OTHER VERY DESPERATE MEASURES HERE:

- ______________________________
- ______________________________
- ______________________________
- ______________________________
- ______________________________
- ______________________________
- ______________________________

Love ~ #5
~ POTION

SIGNS OF NORMAL GRIEF VS. SIGNS OF ABNORMAL GRIEF

STAYING CLASSY LIKE HEIDI KLUM AFTER HER SPLIT FROM SEAL.

FEELING EXHAUSTED AND UNABLE TO CONCENTRATE.

LISTENING TO THE WORLD'S SADDEST MUSIC ON REPEAT.

WHEN LITERALLY
EVERYTHING
REMINDS YOU OF
HIM / HER.

"I REMEMBER
HE/SHE ONCE
SAID HE/SHE
LIKED PINE TREES."

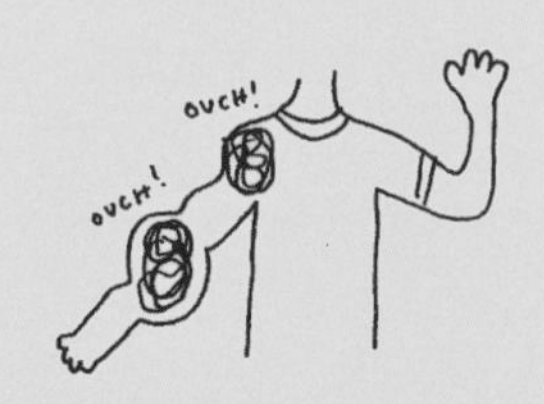

MISSING HIM/HER SO
SO MUCH THAT
IT PHYSICALLY HURTS.

SITTING DOWN
IN THE SHOWER
AND CRYING

FEELING LIKE
YOU'RE MISSING
AN ARM.

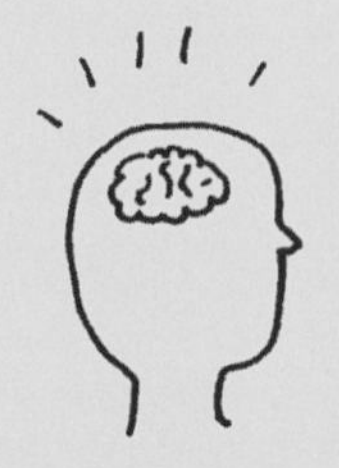

HAVING A
HEADACHE.

FEELING LIKE QUEEN VICTORIA AFTER THE DEATH OF PRINCE ALBERT.

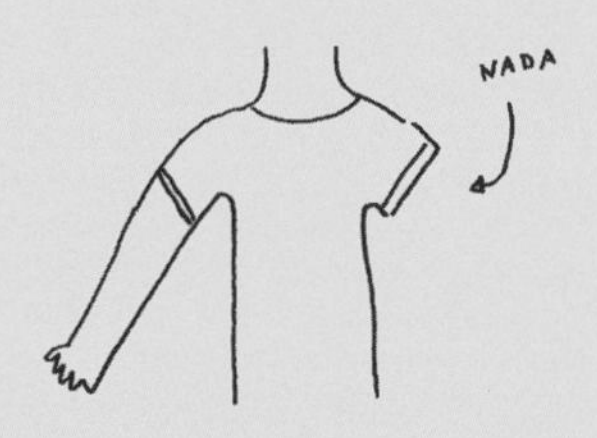

LOSING SENSATION IN YOUR LEFT ARM (COULD BE EITHER A FAKE HEART ATTACK OR A REAL ONE).

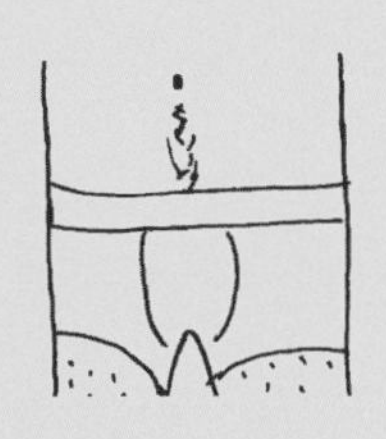

WEARING THE BOXERS/PANTIES THAT HE/SHE LEFT AT YOUR PLACE.

FEELING AS THOUGH LIFE DOESN'T MAKE SENSE WITHOUT HIM/HER. (YOU'RE NOT CONJOINED TWINS.)

NOT CRYING. 

MAKING MATTERS WORSE BY PUTTING YOURSELF IN UNNECESSARY SITUATIONS.

HAVING PANIC ATTACKS. (TIME TO GO TO THE DOCTOR!)

MAGICAL THINKING

- It's common to turn to "magical thinking" when you are looking for comfort during times of sadness. And by "magical thinking" I mean having irrational thoughts such as, "If the fan spins twice, it means he/she is thinking of me."

WRITE SOME OF YOUR "MAGICAL THOUGHTS" HERE:

DRAW A FEW MORE HERE:

REFER BACK TO THIS PAGE IN THREE MONTHS AND LAUGH AT YOURSELF, WHICH IS JUST AS GOOD FOR YOUR WELL-BEING AS THERAPY.

Singing super sad/depressing songs is one of the best remedies out there for someone who is brokenhearted. Who likes to sing along to Calvin Harris, J Balvin, or ______________ (insert any artist who plays nothing but party music) when they're feeling blue? NOBODY.

The reason we seek out sad music when we're feeling depressed is NOT because deep down we're all just a bunch of masochists. It's because we want to recognize our pain in someone else's words. When we identify with song lyrics, we are better able to understand our own feelings, and eventually overcome them.

Listening to sad music at times like this helps us own our emotions, relive moments (music is a way to travel through time), and distract ourselves.

Here is a list of songs from all genres of music that have the power to bring us to tears (beyond the ones you've already cried):

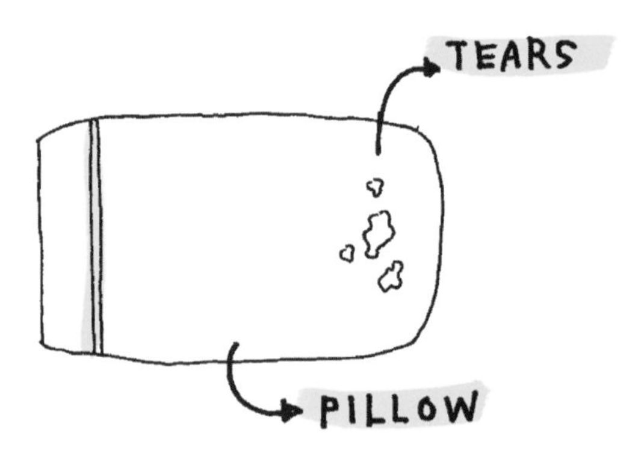

SONGS TO SING IN THE SHOWER

(A LIFE-CHANGING PLAYLIST, SORT OF)

INSTRUCTIONS:
Have this playlist ready in case of emergency. Use during a personal outburst of repressed emotions, or when a friend or family member has a broken heart and you don't know what to say. In the latter case, simply hand them the list along with a pair of "crying sunglasses," which are simply a pair of big, super dark sunglasses that allow you to tear up in the middle of the afternoon without (ALMOST) anyone noticing it.

- ☐ "Torn" – Natalie Imbruglia
- ☐ "Youth" – Daughter
- ☐ "Skinny love" – Bon Iver
- ☐ "We Belong Together" – Mariah Carey
- ☐ "Breathe Me" – Sia
- ☐ "Linger" – The Cranberries
- ☐ "Stay With Me" – Sam Smith
- ☐ "King of Sorrow" — Sade
- ☐ "Nothing Compares 2U" – Sinéad O'Connor
- ☐ "Glory Box" — Portishead
- ☐ "Exit Music (For a Film)" – Radiohead
- ☐ "Love Is a Losing Game" – Amy Winehouse
- ☐ "Thinking Bout You" – Frank Ocean
- ☐ "I'd Rather Go Blind" – Etta James

- ☐ "Honey Honey" – Feist
- ☐ "Everybody Hurts" – R.E.M.
- ☐ "Against All Odds" – The Postal Service
- ☐ "Flinch" – Alanis Morissette
- ☐ "Back to Black" – Amy Winehouse
- ☐ "Walk Away" – Ben Harper
- ☐ "Emotion" – Destiny's Child
- ☐ "Don't Speak" – No Doubt
- ☐ "Ain't No Sunshine" – Bill Withers
- ☐ "Hurt" – Johnny Cash
- ☐ "Someone Like You" – Adele
- ☐ "Best Thing I Never Had" – Beyoncé
- ☐ "Stay" – Rihanna featuring Mikky Ekko
- ☐ "We Are Never Ever Getting Back Together" – Taylor Swift

YOUR PERSONAL PLAYLIST

(In case you think my taste in music sucks, or in case you just want to add to the list.)

- [ ] ____________________
- [ ] ____________________
- [ ] ____________________
- [ ] ____________________
- [ ] ____________________
- [ ] ____________________
- [ ] ____________________

HEALING RITUALS

No more crying. It's time to get better.

RITUAL #1

Print the Gloria Gaynor mantra *Oh no, not I, I will survive* on a small piece of paper. Then laminate it and stick it in your wallet. This ritual amounts to a promise that everything is gonna be okay.

→ If you don't want to print anything, feel free to use the following page.

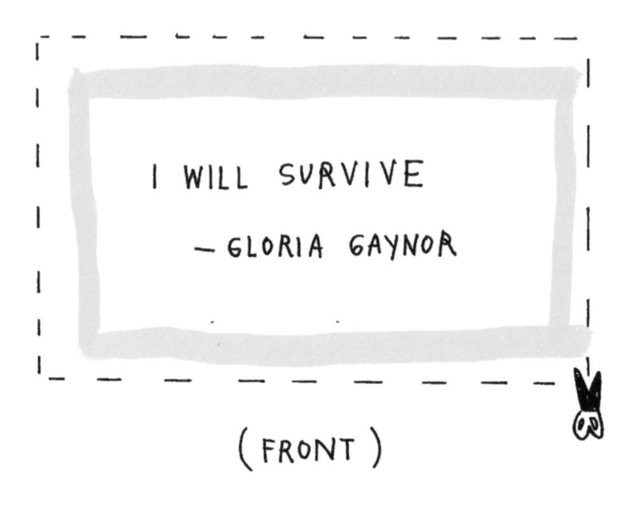
I WILL SURVIVE
– GLORIA GAYNOR

(FRONT)

INSTANT DEPRESSION
CURE TICKET

(BACK)

RITUAL #2

Take a piece of paper and write down all the things that make you sad, the things you want to change, the things you'd like to say but for whatever reason can't. Then light the paper on fire, leaving only ashes. Next, create a potion out of these ashes and give it to the person who has done you wrong, along with a few hairs and a pinch of garden soil.*

* Actually, don't. Just burn the paper. Sending bad vibes up in flames means letting them go, transforming them, converting them into something majestic.
If you're still considering that potion thing, that's a bad sign. You might need more time to heal before moving on to the next stage.

RITUAL #3

Take a few minutes to think about all the negative thoughts or pessimistic ideas you keep repeating to yourself in your head. This voice is what I like to call "La Loca" (that crazy person in your head). This isn't an Eckhart Tolle book and I'm not going to theorize about how deep down "La Loca" is really your ego, but you have to believe me when I say that voice isn't your own. The less you listen to it, the happier you'll be.

NOTE: Don't judge the crazy thoughts no matter how weird/self-hating/pessimistic they sound, just allow those thoughts to come and go.

This ritual consists of drawing a picture of "La Loca" and the things it says to you. In doing so, you're stripping it of the power it has over you.

MY NAME IS

____

(WRITE YOUR NAME HERE, OBVIOUSLY.)

AND THIS IS MY LOCA

RITUAL #4

Give in to your guilty pleasures (such as bingeing reality TV, watching YouTube makeup tutorials for more than ten minutes at a time, eating a triple bacon cheeseburger, practicing Backstreet Boys or Britney Spears dance routines, reciting the Kardashians' kids' names by memory or whatever makes you happy). This ritual is all about instant gratification.

RITUAL #5

Read:

THE HISTORY OF LOVE by Nicole Krauss

OH, THE PLACES YOU'LL GO! by Dr. Seuss

PAPI by Rita Indiana

THE YEAR OF MAGICAL THINKING by Joan Didion

BEFORE NIGHT FALLS by Reinaldo Arenas

UMAMI by Laia Jufresa

A BREATH OF LIFE by Clarice Lispector

YES PLEASE by Amy Poehler

THERE'S A
YOU-SHAPED
HOLE IN MY
HEART

CHAPTER

IT'S NOT TO OKAY

FIVE

OKAY BE

Finding well-being and satisfaction in life no matter the circumstances.

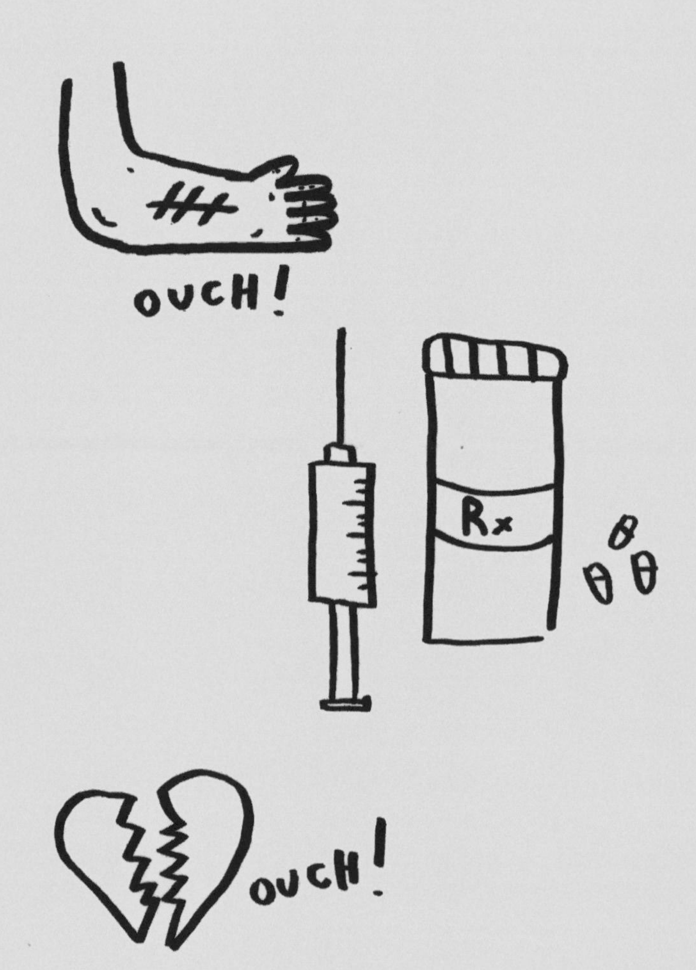
OUCH!
Rx
OUCH!

I always assumed that your ankle was a round bone/joint that sits there where your leg ends and your foot begins. Where the tibia and fibula connect with the navicular bone. I know what the navicular bone is, and I know that the ankle is much more than a round, pointy bone, because my friend's brother destroyed his. When my friend looked at the X-rays after the initial surgery, she asked the doctor, "What's going on here with this hole?" "That hole is the ankle your brother no longer has," the doctor replied.

The ankle is a joint that is made up of three bones: the fibula, the tibia, and the talus, all of which come together with the help of ligaments, tendons, and muscles in a way that allows for movement.

In terms of the biomechanics of the tibiofibular joint complex, when you're making a specific movement (such as pushing the ball of the foot down so you can tiptoe through the house without making any sound, or running across a cold floor at three in the morning in the middle of a dream so you can go pee), a series of small, simultaneous, and opposing movements allow you (or anyone else) to walk stealthily. There is a contraction in the posterior tibialis anterior muscle, a rotation of the lateral malleolus, an extension of the ligament fibers, and so on.

I know this not just because of what happened to Juliana's brother's ankle. I know it because the accident that destroyed his ankle happened two days after the death of La Mamma (I have, or had, two moms: my mother-mom and my aunt-mom-object-of-all-my-love-and-admiration, my anchor, the reason I write).

Since my body still aches when I come to grips with the fact that I'll never be able to touch her hand again, I decided it would be easier to think about someone else's ankle.

My friend says that she understood how serious an accident it was when she felt a pain in her own leg, her own ankle. A phantom pain, something transferred from one to another. A pain that speaks of the bond between her and her brother.

I, too, feel pain and emptiness. I also walk with those spectral feelings. With the sensation of a limb that I no longer have but is nevertheless still there.

We're both hurting, but like I told my friend, that's okay. The pain in her brother's ankle and the death of La Mamma is like that phantom limb: something we no longer have but will never stop feeling.

SOMETIMES IT'S BETTER TO EMBRACE YOUR PAIN THAN TO FIGHT IT.

PEOPLE WHO UNDERSTAND THAT CATASTROPHE CAN LEAD TO VICTORY

ADELE

FIFTEEN GRAMMYS AND COUNTING. INTERNATIONAL ACCLAIM. A NEW LOVE.

SAM SMITH

IN THE LONELY HOUR, AN ALBUM THAT WENT ON TO BE A CHART-TOPPING SUCCESS, WAS BORN OF AN UNREQUITED LOVE.

TAYLOR SWIFT

THE ALBUM *RED* SOLD 1.2 MILLION COPIES IN A SINGLE WEEK.

SOPHIE CALLE

EXQUISITE PAIN AND "TAKE CARE OF YOURSELF" HAVE BEEN EXHIBITED IN TEN DIFFERENT COUNTRIES.

JOAN DIDION

IN *THE YEAR OF MAGICAL THINKING* SHE TRANSFORMED HER PAIN INTO ONE OF THE MOST POWERFUL AND BEAUTIFUL BOOKS EVER WRITTEN.

JEANETTE WINTERSON

TOOK ALL HER CHILDHOOD BAD MEMORIES AND TURNED THEM INTO ART BOOKS IN *ORANGES ARE NOT THE ONLY FRUIT* OR *WHY BE HAPPY WHEN YOU COULD BE NORMAL?*

COLOR-CODED MAP OF PAINS IN MY BODY

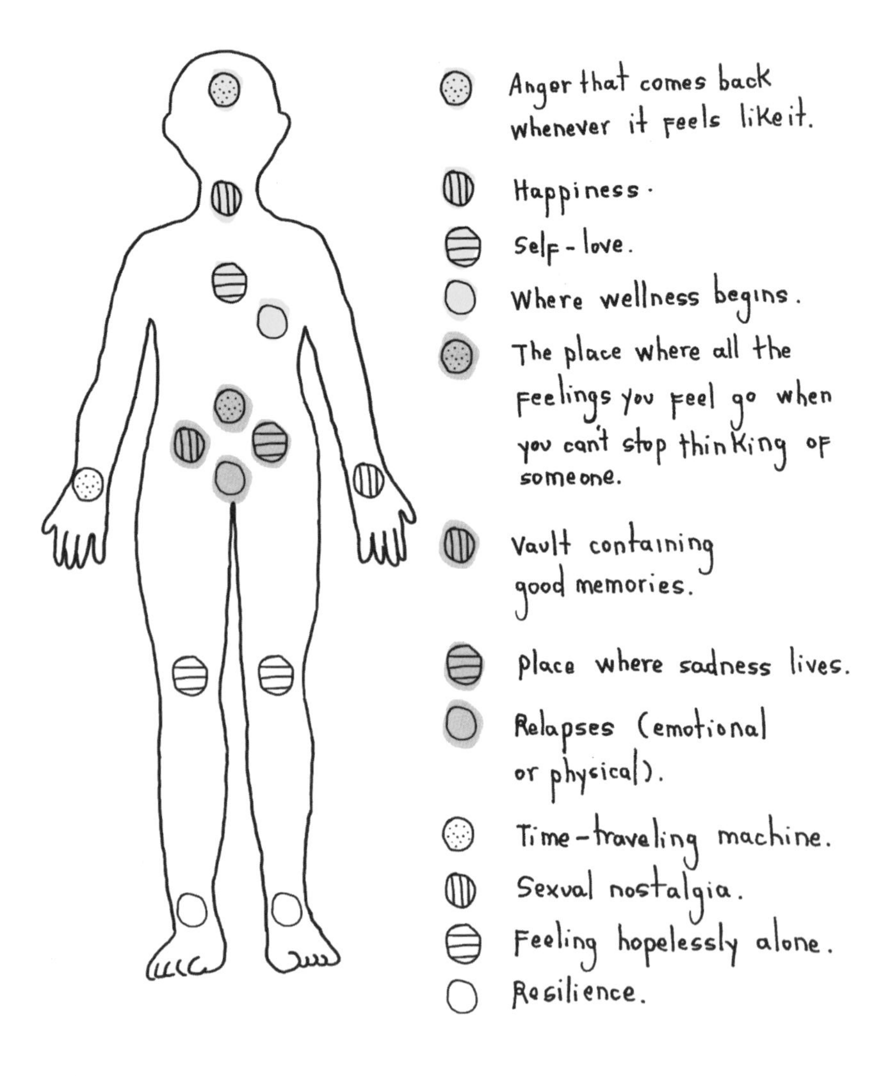

COLOR-CODED MAP OF PAINS IN YOUR BODY

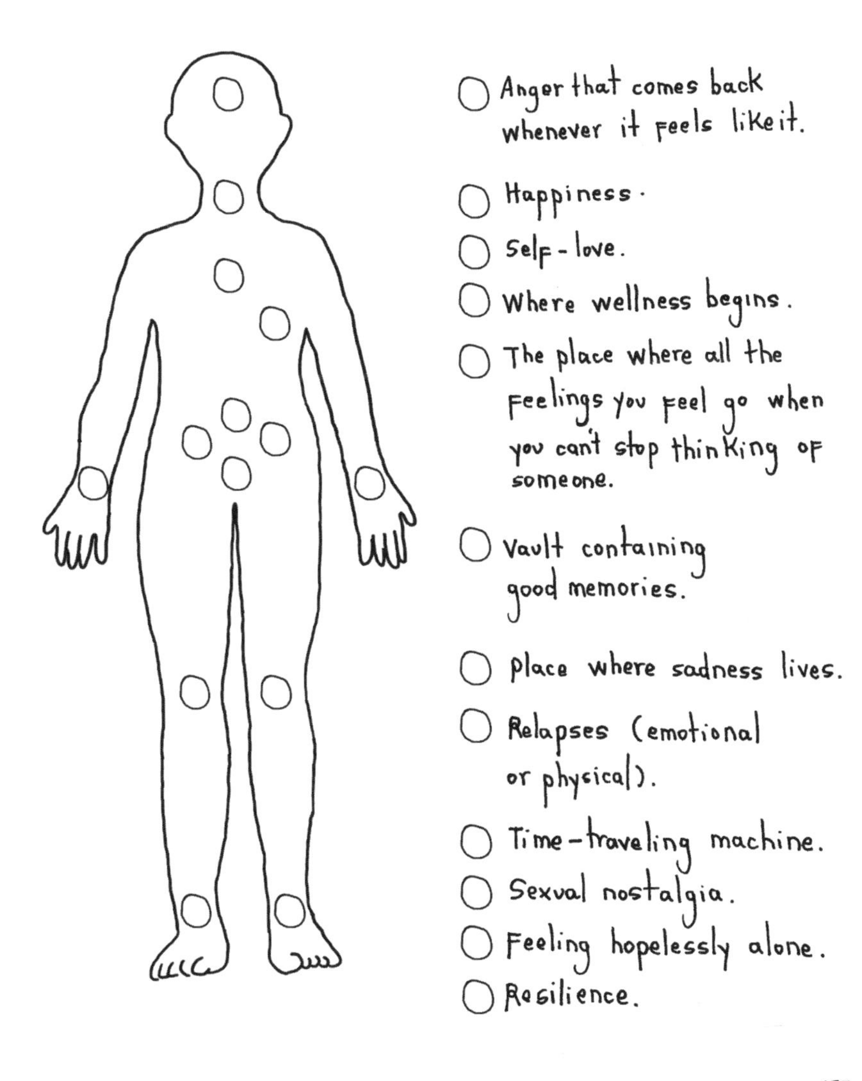

IT'S OKAY NOT TO BE OKAY

We live in an age that glorifies happiness and well-being... just look at any Instagram feed. Still, though, it's really important to remember that IT'S OKAY NOT TO BE OKAY. If you want to sit around for a couple of months and sing "Un-Break My Heart" by Toni Braxton, that's fine. If you want to start exercising and literally run your sorrows into the ground, do it. Everything is on the table. There's no rush and no right way to deal with grief.

Be that as it may, keep the following things in mind when it comes to your own healing process:

- These things take time.
- The rain won't fall forever.
- Bad news: everything changes.
- Good news: everything changes.
- Things could always be worse (unless you're living an Édith Piaf kind of life, in which case I don't know what to tell you).
- One day you'll laugh about all of this. I promise.
- ______________________________
- ______________________________

WRITE YOURSELF A FEW WORDS OF ENCOURAGEMENT.

- COPY OR CUT OUT THIS PAGE AND STICK IT TO THE DOOR OF YOUR REFRIGERATOR.

ACCEPTANCE IS A SUPERPOWER YOU DON'T KNOW YOU HAVE.

To activate this superpower, all you have to do is:

- Forget about denial.
- Accept things for what they truly are.
- Live in the now.
- Be honest with yourself.
- Make loving yourself your top priority.
- Transfer $ 3,000 to checking account # 300947-2601. Kidding! Kidding: I'm not kidding.

Once your superpower has been activated, you will be able to:

- Fly… far away from pain and self-sabotage.
- Keep the situation in perspective. In other words, you'll basically have X-ray vision.
- Be impervious… to bad situations.
- Be invisible… to people who might want to cause you harm.
- Have a selective memory. In other words, you'll be able to turn bad memories into good ones.
- Use rhizomatic thinking. This is the ability to understand that the grieving process isn't linear, nor does it conform to any regular order. Instead, it takes a very irregular path – it rises and falls, and there are neutral spaces as well – where any particular element can point to or otherwise affect any other.

OTHER SUPERPOWERS

THE POWER TO ALWAYS FALL IN LOVE WITH THE MOST EXPENSIVE THING IN A STORE.

Do whatever you feel like doing, but DON'T CALL HER.

THE POWER TO GIVE ADVICE TO OTHERS BUT NOT APPLY IT TO YOURSELF.

THE POWER TO IMMEDIATELY IDENTIFY SONGS LIKE A HUMAN SHAZAM. (IN MY CASE, HOWEVER, THIS POWER ONLY APPLIES TO SADE AND BEYONCÉ.)

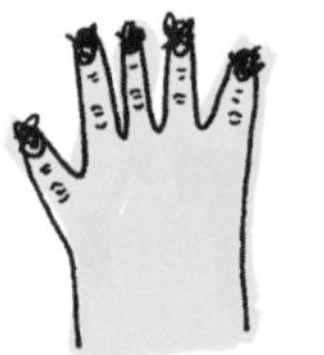

THE POWER TO PAINT YOUR NAILS AS BADLY AS EVER.

Use this space to create a list of YOUR OWN PERSONAL SUPERPOWERS and use them whenever you're feeling down:

SUPERPOWER #1

SUPERPOWER #2

SUPERPOWER #3

SUPERPOWER #4

INSTRUCTIONS FOR TAKING A GEOGRAPHIC PATH TO WELLNESS

Draw a picture of yourself at whichever point along the following line corresponds to your emotional state. Write down the date and a word or two that resonates with your feelings. Use the line as a visual diary of your progress.

NOTE: For best results, rotate the book 90 degrees to the right. ⟶

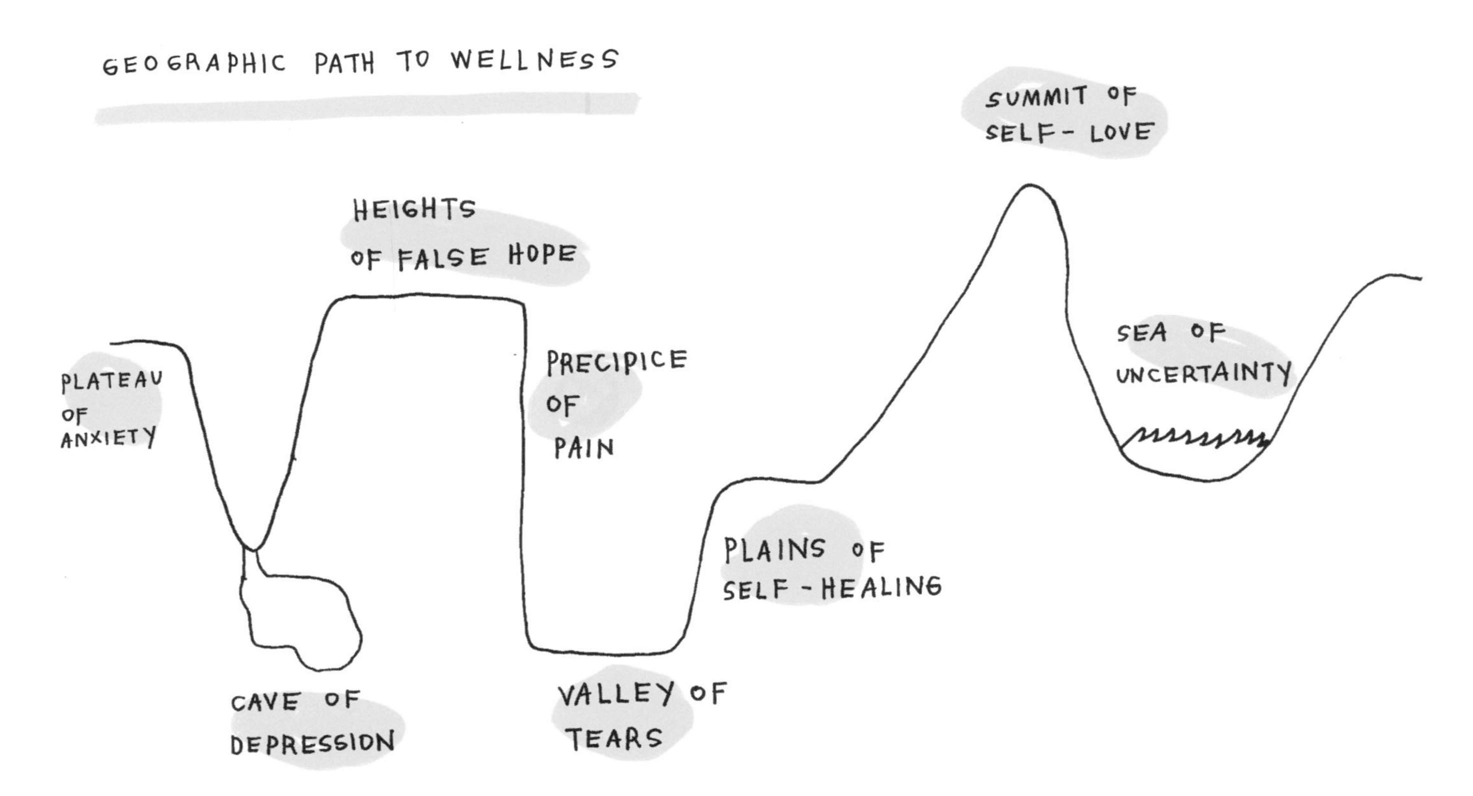
GEOGRAPHIC PATH TO WELLNESS
PLATEAU OF ANXIETY
CAVE OF DEPRESSION
HEIGHTS OF FALSE HOPE
PRECIPICE OF PAIN
VALLEY OF TEARS
PLAINS OF SELF-HEALING
SUMMIT OF SELF-LOVE
SEA OF UNCERTAINTY

CHAPTER

REINVE YOUR

SIX

NTING SELF

The act of dying and being reborn. Self-replication with Improved Emotional Results.

We're all broken. Everybody is. Without exception. Isabel is twenty-eight years old and can't sleep alone because she says she hears voices. I tell her they aren't voices, they're her own thoughts, things that have to be said even if she doesn't want to hear them. She's afraid of loneliness: of falling one morning in the shower and lying there as the water washes over her, of remaining there, motionless and naked, having surrendered herself to the fall without so much as a hint of dignity, of days and days going by before anyone starts to worry about her, of whether she'll die before the icy flow of water ends. Isabel knows that this would be the cruelest form of torture, not so much because of the temperature of the water but because of the eternity of the fall.

I tell her that what she fears is silence. Unspoken words. Invisible things, unreadable things, untranslatable things. Our fears aren't written in silence. It's the truths we do not want to see that are written there because we don't feel as though we deserve them. These are the truths that can make us great, but often we choose not to grow into them because we're hesitant to accept the fact that we are infinite and can do anything.

Laura has panic attacks when crossing the street. They started out harmless enough, but now they're overwhelming. She has to ask strangers for help when crossing big avenues. She grips their sweaty hands, closes her eyes tight, and lets herself go. *Everything's gonna be okay, everything's gonna be okay*, she repeats to herself. *You just have to get from one side to the other*. She doesn't know why this happens, but when she sees the cars speeding down the avenue, all she can think about is being run over by one of those metallic demolition machines.

María can no longer have an orgasm without immediately feeling an overwhelming wave of sadness, a void that makes her feel empty inside. Nobody knows this. It's a pain that she chokes down and hides behind silence or kisses or forgetfulness, or all three.

I'm broken, too. I think a lot before I fall asleep. I spend long periods of time living in the thresholds. I have many more fears than I'm willing to admit. My knees hurt, as do my feet and my back. Yes, especially my back.

We are all full of borders. We all walk around with our wounds to the right and our joys to the left. But these wounds always heal. Being broken is what allows us to steel ourselves at a moment's notice. Living in a state of continuous death enables us to constantly reinvent ourselves, to shake off the fears and pains that have attached themselves to our bodies and be reborn.

NEW THINGS GROW FROM
OLD WOUNDS AS THEY HEAL.

SOMETIMES I RUN,
SOMETIMES I ~~HIDE~~
HIKE.

EVERYTHING CHANGES

One morning you'll wake up singing happy songs and you'll dance in your pajamas. You'll enjoy the feeling of being a new person. You'll feel sick and tired of lying in bed all day. You'll want to go out and write or draw or do whatever else you might feel like doing. And that's the day when you'll begin to reinvent yourself, when you'll have the chance to be who you really want to be.

Here is a list of ideas, activities, and exercises to help maintain this renewed feeling that life really isn't always ~~a bitch~~ so bad.

NUMBER ONE

PHYSICAL ACTIVITIES

CLIMB MOUNTAINS

AT DAWN.

BREAK OUT THE ROLLERBLADES THAT HAVE BEEN SITTING IN YOUR CLOSET FOR THE PAST TWELVE YEARS.

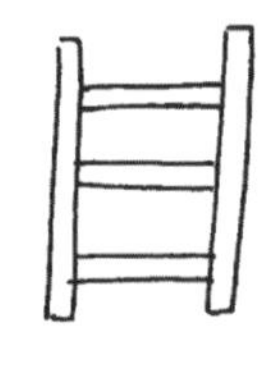

CLIMB STAIRS.

GO FOR A RUN.

NUMBER TWO

NEW PROFESSIONAL HORIZONS

BECOME A PROFESSIONAL ENAMELIST (A PERSON WHO STUDIES, CREATES, AND NAMES NAIL POLISH).

BECOME A SHADOWBOXER.

BECOME A CAT WALKER.

BECOME A STORM CHASER.

NUMBER THREE

SPIRITUALITY

TAKE UP YOGA.

MEDITATE.

(BELIEVE IT OR NOT, DOING THE DISHES COUNTS AS MEDITATION.)

RECITE MANTRAS

Nam-myoho-renge-kyo: embrace and manifest your Buddha nature.

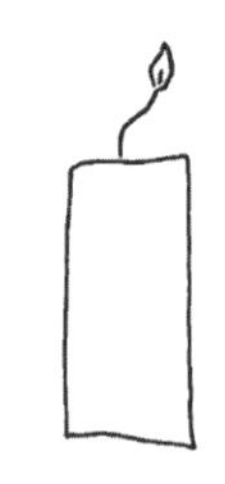

LIGHT CANDLES.

NUMBER FOUR

FUN ACTIVITIES

SING ALONG TO MICHAEL JACKSON IN THE LIVING ROOM.

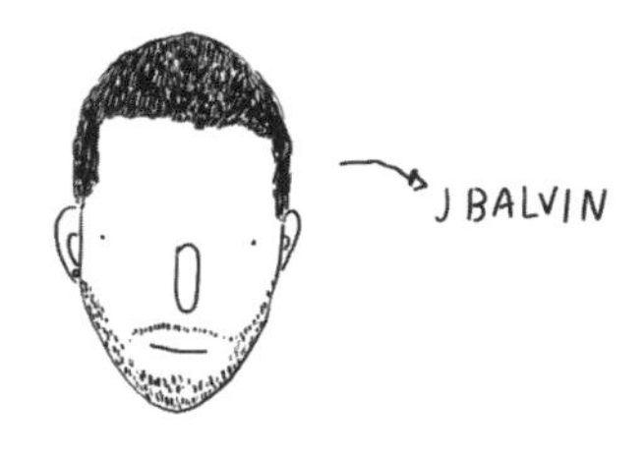

BURN CALORIES BY DANCING TO REGGAETON (ESPECIALLY "GINZA" BY J BALVIN).

SEND HANDWRITTEN LETTERS TO YOUR BEST FRIENDS.

LAURYN HILL

MEMORIZE RAP LYRICS— TRY "DOOWOP (THAT THING)" BY LAURYN HILL.

NUMBER FIVE

HEALTHY EATING HABITS

JUICING

SUPERFOODS

PESCETARIANISM

(also Known as '80s vegetarianism, or being a vegetarian except for eating Fish)

GLUTEN-FREE

Gluten is the Pablo Escobar of a new generation. Nobody can see it, but everyone is afraid of it.

NUMBER SIX

TURN A LIFE EXPERIENCE INTO AN ARTISTIC OR CREATIVE WORK (LIKE THIS BOOK)

FILL THIS SPACE WITH WRITING/ DRAWINGS/ IDEAS THAT YOU WILL LATER TURN INTO PROJECTS.

CHAPTER

WHEN TEARS GONE

SEVEN

THE ARE

A (Fictitious) Biography of
João Pedro de Almeida Santos Abreu,
(Fictional) Composer of the Lambada.

JOÃO'S
FUTURE

It all started when something stirred deep inside of her. "This can't be good," Rita de Almeida Santos Abreu thought as she washed her underwear in the shower. The place: a poorhouse north of Salvador de Bahía, Brazil, where Rita lived with her uncle who was deaf in one ear. The year: 1968.

Things that happened in 1968:

- James Earl Ray assassinated Martin Luther King Jr.

- Yoko Ono wrote a love letter to John Lennon. (Unbeknownst to them, this letter would be forever lost in the sea of dead mail sent through the U.S. Postal Service.)

- The dictator Artur da Costa e Silva decreed Institutional Act 5, thus turning Brazil into an unlivable country.

The color of the sky that morning: blue. The color of the underwear Rita was washing: pink. What had happened a week before: Rita had slept with Abel, her boyfriend for the past seven months, for the last time.

Abel was twenty-one and Rita was fifteen. Abel liked to play soccer, drink warm beer, lounge around, and sleep with Rita. Rita, on the other hand, liked to dance. She wanted to become a famous actress, and she believed her dreams were like a superpower that would take her far away, wherever she wanted to go, past the Baltic islands, past Japan, past the blue or sometimes purple skies over Salvador de Bahía.

Rita loved Abel, but she knew he was no good for her, and that if she stayed with him she'd end up living with her deaf uncle in one room and Abel and his warm beers in another while she spent her days working double shifts at a hospital or airport or country club and getting home so late at night that she'd begin to forget about her dreams. If she stayed with him, she'd never become a famous actress; instead she would become the star of the local theater group, which would name a poor ugly building after her exactly one year and three days after she passed away. That wouldn't be such a bad thing; it just wasn't what she truly wanted. Rita knew all of this—how Abel was a disaster waiting to happen, how she could get stuck in a life she loathed forever, how that ugly building could have her name painted in green just outside the porch—with the same certainty that she knew her name was Rita, that river water had curative powers, and that the grass wasn't always greener on the other side of the fence. So she decided to sleep with Abel one last time that night and say goodbye without really saying goodbye.

She made love slowly at first and then stronger, with her heart in his skin and desire in her hands: the same desire she had felt—and would continue to feel—for him since the very first time she saw him near the beach, when Abel hugged her around her waist and said, "Don't go, stay here with me."

Eight months and three weeks after that day she was washing her pink underwear in the shower, João Pedro de Almeida Santos Abreu—the thing that had been stirring deep inside of her—was born.

João inherited the same name as his deaf grandfather, the same bad luck with love as Rita, and the same taste for warm beer as Abel, whom he would never meet. Rita refused to tell Abel about João's existence, and she wouldn't tell João about Abel's existence either. But around the time the child turned five, his father finally learned that he had a son and spent many nights standing outside their house, drunkenly ranting, "I am your dad. THIS MAN STANDING OUTSIDE YOUR HOUSE IS YOUR FATHER!"

When João asked his mother if what this drunk

man said was true, Rita simply answered with "Everyone believes what they want to believe."

But after João had asked her that question, Rita knew that eventually they would have to leave.

The day Uncle Grandpa died, Rita packed up their things, took João by the hand, and left for Río to become the famous actress she had always dreamed of being. Before getting into the taxi, João slipped a piece of paper under the front door that read:

DEAR MR. DRUNK MAN WHO SHOUTS IN THE STREET AT NIGHT SAYING HE'S MY FATHER:

We're moving to Río. Here is our adress. Come visit me.

Rua Marquês de São Vicente
496, Gâvea
CEP 22457-040
Río de Janeiro / RJ

RÍO
21 YEARS LATER

Abel never visited. On the day of his twenty-first birthday, João left home and headed off to the university, ready to present one of his theories on the science of human emotions he had been working on in his downtime during the cold nights of June when his mother was rehearsing her scripts.

João had grown up alone, without any real friends, and—as you might have expected—without ever having fallen in love.

Between auditions for telenovelas (which took up so much of Rita's time that she was always out of the house, returning home at random hours like 1:45 a.m. or 2:02 p.m.), João's mother occasionally remembered that she had a son and would blurt out something like "Get your nose out of those textbooks and go find yourself a girlfriend." Then, almost immediately, it was as if João went back to being invisible to Rita while she proceeded to rant angrily about Brazilian television, the production manager, the lead actor's bad breath, the food on set and how it was making her hair fall out, the screenwriters, and her failing dreams. Rita didn't want to be just a costar on an evening telenovela. Rita wanted to be a Hollywood star, win an Oscar, and live in a mansion with two golden lions guarding the entrance.

She was motivated by her own dissatisfaction, and—as we all know—chronic dissatisfaction is a deadly virus.

João's dream was to become the Carl Sagan of Affective Events, and he was absolutely convinced that the study he was about to present in class that day would revolutionize the field and make him a world-renowned theorist. But that never happened.

On the bus to campus, sitting in the second row of seats, was Aurora.

Aurora was nineteen years old, she secretly liked to eat toothpaste, and she wanted to become a doctor. I could say that what happened between them was love at first sight. But that—aside from being a horrible cliché—would amount to only half of the truth.

Here's what happened: João saw Aurora and fell in love with her. He knew this because he ended up chatting about the weather or current political events until the bus driver came to the very end of his route and made them get off in the middle of nowhere. That's why he never presented his revolutionary theory on Affective Events: a decision that he would regret for the rest of his life.

Aurora saw João and thought that she might end up falling in love with him. But more than that: she wanted to give it a try.

What happened next could be called *João Pedro de Almeida Santos Abreu's Story of Love and Loss*, which were the best and worst things that ever happened in his life.

After that day, João and Aurora met every morning to have breakfast together and every night to read. For him, it was books on quantum physics and Freud, while for her, it was *Grey's Anatomy*. At first, João doubted his feelings because as a theorist he had no other preexistent feeling for which to compare his current feelings for Aurora. For him, love was a suspicious thing, and at the same time, in a sweet contradictory coexistence, a certainty. But eventually there came a simple moment of complete and resounding clarity for him where he knew that being in love was a sum of indescribable simple gestures: Aurora's hand on his leg as they sat on the bus, the way the white T-shirt his mother once gave him now clung to her body as they walked together along the beach, the secrets she whispered in his ear, the bits of toothpaste she gave him through kisses and that he welcomed like candy passed from tongue to tongue.

Aurora always thought that she could fall in love with João, but that day never came, because no matter how much you want to, love doesn't work like a virus. Love is nontransferable, love is individual. Two people will never feel quite the same love for each other, even if they spend a lifetime trying.

João knew this, just as he knew from the very beginning that things were going to end badly. But that still didn't stop him from forgetting everything else and making Aurora his world. Aurora, however, tired of not feeling anything, started screwing several friends plus a bunch of strangers simply to feel alive. João found out about this, but wasn't able to leave her. Aurora thought that maybe his pain would bring her closer to him, but this, sadly, did not happen either.

Once, at his one and only true friend's birthday party, João caught Aurora in a compromising position with Luis, the birthday boy, in a dark corner near the pavilion by the pool. He went back home and sat on the edge of the bed for an hour, two hours, five hours, or more. He just sat there without moving. All he could think about was the two of them: the two of them against a backdrop of subtle moaning, while he stood there in absolute silence. The feeling that his life was fading away, the trembling in his knees, the dull pain, the nausea, the dizziness. He didn't know exactly how much time had passed since he saw them together. Maybe eight hours, maybe less. When she finally got home, Rita asked him what was wrong. "Nothing," João said.

That wasn't true.

Dear Aurora:

It already hurts. It hurts a lot.
It hurts in my ~~sto~~ stomach, in
my lips. My hands are shaking
constantly. Everything is. I can't
sleep. I cry uncontrollably I'm
trying to control myself. I'm
trying to hold it together. But
I can't. All I can do is bawl
and wail... These sounds seem
ripped out of some place I didn't
know existed until today, until
yesterday. Like my grief has
been born of a pain
so deep, so wide, so intense,
so cruel that it's just unspeakable,
inconceivable. Not even the worst
adjectives on earth could ever come
close to describing how ~~I'm~~ I'm
feeling. Not even words like
horrifying, maddening, terrible,
terrifying, hideous.

João.

João wrote that letter but he never delivered it. He simply could not honestly embody or convey his true feelings. He cried so much he thought he might die, and after many months of neither sleeping nor eating, of thinking about how the world didn't make any sense, he finally remembered his forgotten theory on Affective Events, the power of neurolinguistics, and its resemblance to sorcery.

The pain he felt was so great that he simply couldn't experience anything else. He thought that all he needed was to get past that initial state of shock so that both his body and his mind could realize that what he'd seen was true and thus begin to feel more. And the sooner the pain begins, he figured, the sooner it will end.

He sat down to write and write and write. After two months of this, the result was a song that made the days of neurolinguistic programming seem distant: a spell that had the power to make Aurora cry just by hearing it, regardless of where she was or how she was feeling.

"Chorando Se Foi," also known as the Lambada. A song, a mechanism of psycho-emotional manipulation so effective that—to this very day—whenever someone sings it at a faraway wedding, Aurora feels a pain in the pit of her stomach and a sense of sadness sweeping over her body.

This was his revenge: João, who would never fall in love again, never write another paper on Affective Events.

Today, João lives in a remote village in Chile. He's a millionaire thanks to the royalties he's earned from that song. They say he's famous as far away as Zimbabwe, and that someone, someday, will make a documentary about his life. A documentary that will change the lives of everyone who sees it but his own. A documentary that will go on to win the Oscar that Rita never did.

THEORY OF AFFECTIVE NON-RETURN

A Thesis on Positive Psychoactiveness

João Pedro de Almeida Santos Abreu

June 21, 1989

The hardest thing of it all is to begin. After the first step has been taken, all that is required is to let oneself be carried away by the invisible force that pulls everyone and everything forward.

The natural tendency is to grow, to advance. We move from Point A to Point B and then to Point C (see Fig.). And while life is returning us to Point A, after those returns or setbacks, the tendency will always and ever be toward Point D and then Point E followed by F, G, H, I, J, K, L, M, N, O, P, Q, R, S, T, U, V, W, X, Y, and Z.

Mobility between the different essential points is unaffected by the fact that the force driving said movement is, without exception, a positive one.

The conclusion of the theory of affective non-return is that the path forward is the path of least resistance. Going backward, even when necessary, involves a greater expenditure of physical and—above all—emotional energy. It applies as much to time travel into the past as it does to people who enjoy running backward because they feel it will put less stress on their knees.

Living in the past is scientifically and spiritually impossible. Life exists in the here and now.

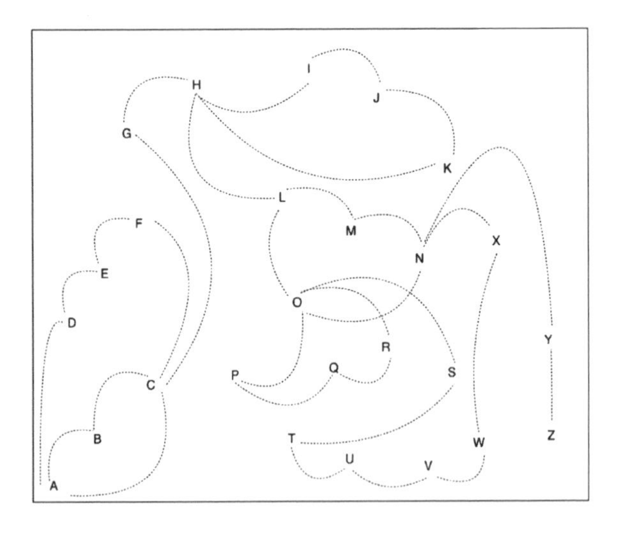

Fig. Map of simple harmonic motion in psychoactive situations involving human beings (DE ALMEIDA SANTOS ABREU, João).

A GUIDE TO FINDING LOVE AFTER HEARTBREAK

Creating a guide for finding your way through a broken heart is easy. When it comes to love, on the other hand, it's almost impossible. why ? We don't really know how to love. What little we do Know about it comes from watching THE LITTLE MERMAID, who trades away her greatest talent – her voice – to cowardly old Ursula in order to be ~~trance~~ transformed into someone she's not so she can go chase after a man she doesn't even Know. That's just not the way to go about it. And if love is such a difficult process, then finding love after heartbreak is even harder. After all, we're still half broken, haunted by our past, and living in a constant state of paranoia about forever suffering through such a profound sadness as the one we're only just now trying to get over.

In order to get past our fears and not make the same mistakes that Ariel did, here is a guide for finding love after heartbreak.*

*GUARANTEED 99.999 PERCENT SUCCESS RATE IF DIRECTIONS ARE FOLLOWED STEP-BY-STEP.

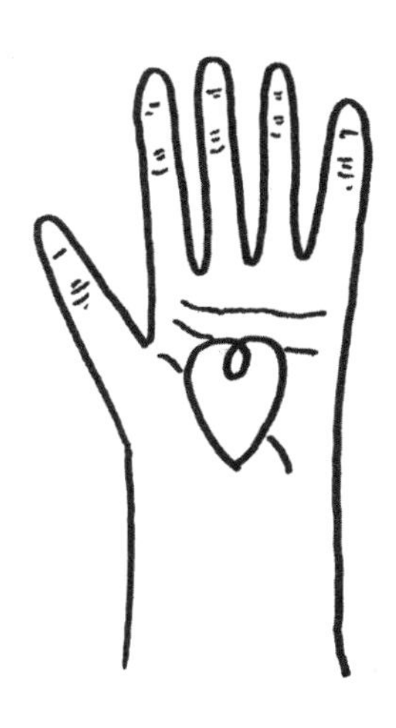

PART ONE: HOW NOT TO LOVE

Love is an individual, nontransferable experience. There are as many different ways to love as there are photos of the Kardashians in the world. Since there really isn't such a thing as a book on how to love the right way, here you have a list of examples of how NOT to do it:

He loves me. He keeps me locked up in a little room. If that's not true love, I don't know what is.

AS UGLY BETTY SAYS TO DON ARMANDO

I'm going to disappear for a month to show you how important you are and how much I love you.

AS F., MY BEST FRIEND'S EX, WOULD SAY

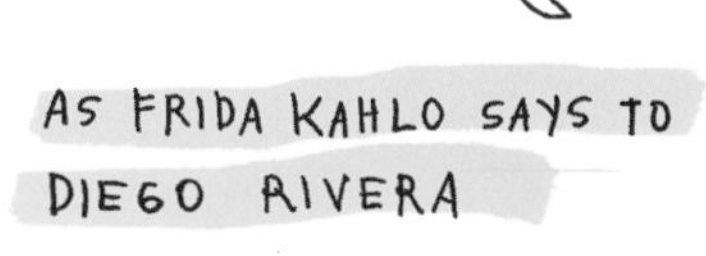

AS FRIDA KAHLO SAYS TO DIEGO RIVERA

Addicted to love? Me? NEVER.

AS ELIZABETH TAYLOR WOULD SAY

USE THIS SPACE TO DRAW A FEW EXAMPLES OF HOW NOT TO LOVE. (FEEL FREE TO INCLUDE EX-BOYFRIENDS/ EX-GIRLFRIENDS, EX-LOVERS, AND EVEN YOURSELF.)

DEAR GOD,
EITHER FIND ME
SOMEONE TO BRING
ME IN OUT OF COLD
NIGHTS, OR END
COLD NIGHTS FOREVER.

PART TWO: JUST LOOKING FOR A LITTLE LOVE

As the great existential philosopher Cher once postulated, "Do you believe in life after love?" In my own personal experience, after my breakup, the answer was a resounding NO. Everything I had ever believed about love had just been demolished. My struggles had been in vain. My disillusionment was just too complete. Not only was it hard to reinvent myself and rebuild my life, but I had also become a complete and total cynic. "Love doesn't exist" was my life's motto for quite some time. I would devote myself to renouncing love forever and finding unconditional love in a Bernese mountain dog puppy I would name Cindy after Cindy Crawford. Cindy was never going to betray me, she would be happy to see me every single day of her life, she wouldn't complain if I didn't wash the dishes, she wouldn't leave me for my ex's ex, and she wouldn't say things like, "It's been a while since you posted a picture of me on Instagram... must mean that you don't love me anymore."

But life has its ways, and a Bernese mountain dog wouldn't fit in my house anyway. So, still carrying a world of fear on my shoulders, I came to realize that what I was looking for wasn't Cindy but a new – and healthier – love.

THIS IS CINDY.* THE BEST ~~PET~~ THING THAT NEVER HAPPENED TO ME. CINDY, I LOVE YOU.

* SEEING A CINDY WALKING DOWN THE STREET IS A SIGN OF GOOD LUCK IN LOVE. IF YOU SEE ONE, TAKE A PICTURE AND UPLOAD IT WITH THE HASHTAG #CINDYBRINGSLOVE.

Here's a list of important prerequisites for when it comes to finding love after heartbreak:

1. Unless you are Taylor Swift, try to dedicate at least a little bit of time to yourself. A broken heart isn't like Zika in the sense that you don't have to sit in quarantine before getting back out there; but at the same time, remember that time cures everything, heals everything, and is capable of (almost) anything.

2. Make sure that your past is where it belongs. And wherever that is, remember you are no longer there yourself (unless you are, in which case, go back and reread this book from the beginning).

3. Love doesnt just appear like Beetlejuice (although it should). If you really want to find someone, you have to work at it. In other words, be ready to go out a lot, meet new people, suffer through a few bad dates, learn to flirt on Tinder (never LinkedIn), and everything else that might seem a bit hellish but will one day prove to be worth it.

4. Not being an expert, I can't really think of anything else to add, but if you can, please feel free to add it here:

____

____

____

____

____

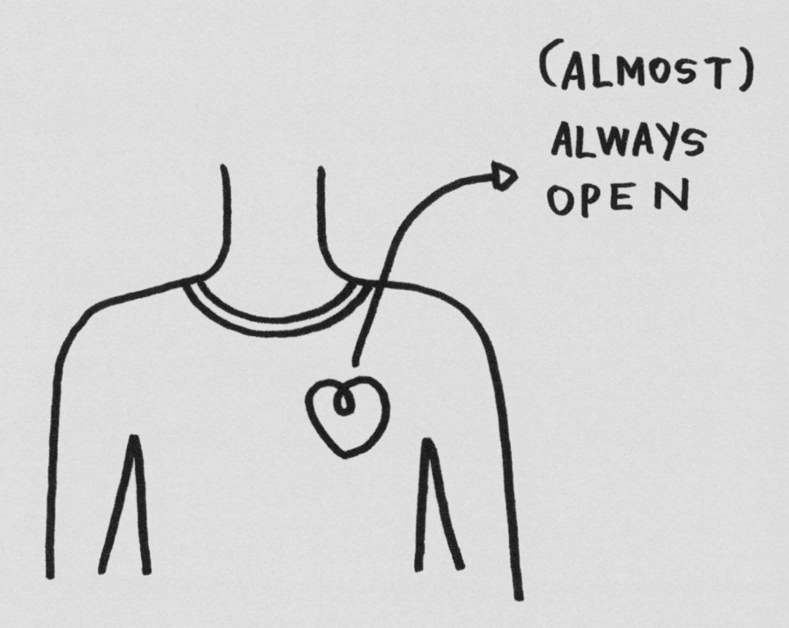
(ALMOST)
ALWAYS
OPEN

PART THREE: THE TRAVEL THEORY

Emotional availability should function like a trip in every sense of the word. You need to open yourself up to new experiences, get out of your comfort zone, be willing to try anything (or almost anything), leave your fears behind, and above all else... just let yourself be free.

I don't know who it was who said love isn't a destination, it's a journey (it was probably Aerosmith or astrologer Susan Miller, or maybe I just made it up myself), but anyway, if you're ready to get back in the love game, using one of these three strategies is a good way to start.

ONE:
VISITING NEW PLACES

In the words of Terry Pratchett, "Why do you go away? So that you can come back. So that you can see the place you came from with new eyes and extra colors. And the people there see you differently, too. Coming back to where you started is not the same as never leaving." – *A Hat Full of Sky*.

There's nothing more therapeutic than a trip. whether it's to Bali or your best friend's house. Traveling helps you get back to yourself, reconnect with what's important, and remember the little things that make you happy. It's also good for meeting new people, because who knows, you might just end up meeting the love of your life at a concert or something.

TWO:

VISITING NEW PEOPLE

This is the part where I say there's no truth to the expression "the best way to get over someone is to get under someone else". Some lovers are right and some lovers are wrong. You should look at meeting new people as a trip in and of itself: one that could end badly, one that could be short and sweet, or — if the planets align, and if Jesus, Mary, and Beyoncé bless it — one that could be transcendent.

Exploring new bodies is fine as long as it's not an excuse for not dealing with the pain, and not a form of escapism.

THE WRONG LOVER

THE RIGHT LOVER

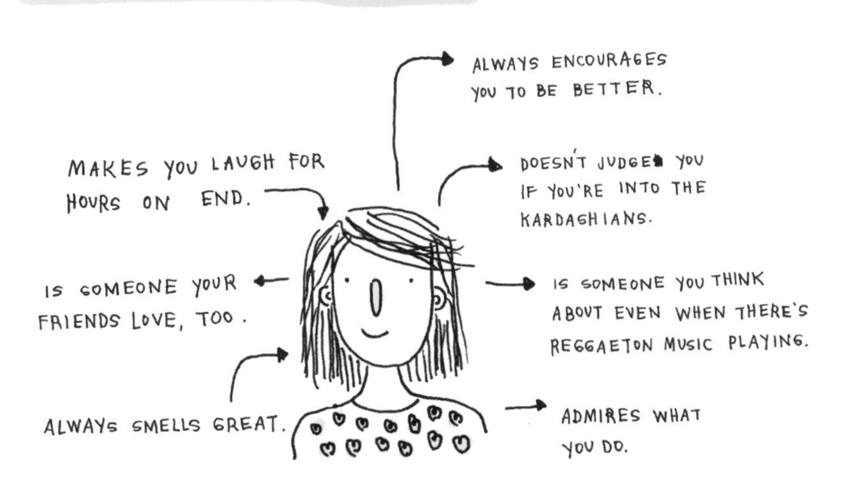

THREE:
VISITING YOURSELF

Actually, this is a trip that shouldn't have to happen. Visiting yourself means trying not to betray yourself and connecting with what it is that makes you you.*

* GOD, PLEASE FORGIVE ME IF THAT SENTENCE SOUNDS LIKE SOMETHING DALE CARNEGIE WOULD HAVE WRITTEN.

PART FOUR: EXPERTS ON LOVE REBORN

People of great emotional wisdom whose lessons for life (often meaning their songs) help us believe in love again and that anything is possible.

SADE
Mother Superior of Emotional Confidence

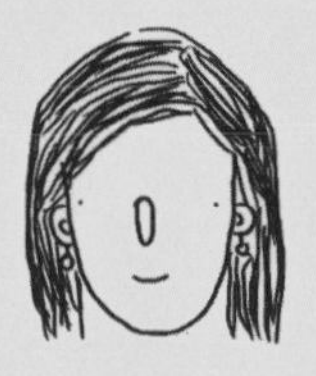

CARRIE FISHER
High Priestess of Love Reborn

"TAKE YOUR BROKEN HEART AND TURN IT INTO ART."

CHIMAMANDA NGOZI ADICHIE
Cardinal of Newfound Hope

"THIS WAS LOVE: A STRING OF COINCIDENCES THAT GATHERED SIGNIFICANCE AND BECAME MIRACLES."

—*Half of a Yellow Sun*

PATERSON
(FROM THE 2016 JIM JARMUSCH FILM *PATERSON*)
Patron Saint of Renewed Optimism
"WITHOUT LOVE, WHAT REASON IS THERE FOR ANYTHING?"

GABRIEL GARCÍA MÁRQUEZ
Prophet of Sensible Love
"IT'S ENOUGH FOR ME TO BE SURE THAT YOU AND I EXIST AT THIS MOMENT."
— *One Hundred Years of Solitude*

PART FIVE: FALLING IN LOVE... WITH YOURSELF

If Jesus said it, it must be true: you can't love someone if you don't first love yourself. It seems easy and even sounds cliché, but God knows it can be one of the hardest things to do, especially if you're dealing with a broken heart, low self-esteem, and overexposure to pics of Kendall Jenner or the many talents of Tina Fey. So here are a few excercises you can do to help that love of self grow:

1. Dedicate a song to yourself (I'm being serious here) and belt it out at least once a day. Recommendations include "The Greatest" by Sia or "Soy Yo" by Bomba Estéreo.

2. Write your own exercise here:

____

____

____

3. Cut out these badges and use them to reward yourself:

PART SIX: FALLING IN LOVE ... WITH SOMEONE ELSE

If you feel you're now ready to venture out there into the world of love again, use these images to help you conquer it, either directly or indirectly (by subtly posting them on Instagram, for example).

WARNING:

- Use with caution.
- Do not attempt to make a new love into everything that a past love was not. Simply let it be.
- Proceed with care: renewed hope can occasionally lead to unexpected behavior and mood swings.
- Remember: just because this new person likes the same toppings on his/her pizza, or the same song from the same band that nobody's ever heard of, it doesn't mean he/she is now the love of your life.

12
3
6
9
NOW IS THE TIME
TO BE HAPPY.

I DON'T NEED
TO BE there
TO BE THERE

ring
call me,
MAY BE

I'M A LITTLE MESSED
UP, BUT YOU LIKE ME
anyway

I FANCY
FANCYING
- YOU -

EVERY love SONG
EVER WRITTEN IS
ABOUT ME (about us)

PART SEVEN: THE ICE CREAM THEORY

It's easy to meet someone new (when everything is going suspiciously well) and feel overwhelmed by paranoid concerns, such as:

- What if this ends?
- Could I be doing this right?
- It's barely just beginning, and I'm already worried about how it's going to end.
- What if the same thing happens all over again?
- Is this normal? What is normal, anyway? Am I normal? Mom, help!

If any of these apply to you (don't worry, yes, it is normal... I think), now is the time to apply the ice cream theory.

THE ICE CREAM THEORY (AS IT APPLIES TO LOVE)

THEORY: Nobody eats an ice cream cone worrying about how it might end. If that were true, nobody would ever eat ice cream.

CONCLUSION: Enjoy your ice cream, and stop overthinking everything.

THE END.

CRYSTAL BALL OF
FUTURE LOVERS

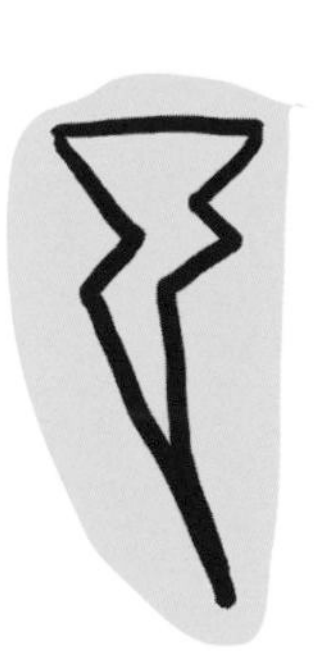

KORN
FLAKES

MILK

RECIPES

ALL SORTS OF DISHES TO HELP HEAL A BROKEN HEART

NOTE: All recipes are the creation of the talented and imaginative chef SILVANA VILLEGAS, the creative mastermind behind MASA, the restaurant and bakery where I wrote much of this book.

Magic Soup That Cures Everything

(Also known as chicken soup with vegetables.)

This magic soup has superpowers invisible to you. It might seem like just a regular chicken soup with vegetables, but if you have a cup each Thursday for a month, your heartbreak symptoms will be reduced by at least 50 percent. Guaranteed by all grandmothers around the globe.

6 servings

Ingredients:

- 1 chicken breast
- 6 cups water
- 1 1/2 teaspoon salt
- 1 pinch black pepper
- 2 cloves minced garlic
- 1 finely chopped red onion
- 1 pat butter
- 1 small carrot, peeled and cubed
- 1/2 cup corn
- 1/3 cup peas
- 1/3 cup chopped green beans
- 1/4 bell pepper, diced

- 1/4 green plantain, peeled and diced
- 3 small fingerling potatoes, peeled and diced
- 1/4 leek, diced
- 10 spinach leaves cut into strips
- 4 sprig of cilantro
- Salt and pepper to taste

Instructions:

1. Put chicken in a pot with six cups of water and a teaspoon of salt.

2. Simmer over medium heat for approximately ten minutes or until fully cooked.

3. Remove the chicken and set the pot of water aside (this will be used later as the soup base). Shred the chicken.

4. Sauté the garlic and red onion in a pan with a pat of butter plus 1/2 teaspoon of salt and a pinch of pepper, then add to the pot.

5. Add the rest of the chopped vegetables, including the potatoes, and plantain, and a sprig of cilantro to the pot. Boil until the carrot and potatoes are soft.

6. Remove the sprig of cilantro and season the soup with salt and pepper.

7. Add the spinach and shredded chicken to the pot.

8. Ladle into bowls, garnish with a bit of chopped cilantro, and serve.

Feeling Feelings Cookies

(Also known as butter cookies.)

This recipe consists of two parts: The first is baking the butter cookies, just like the ones you ate when you were a kid. The second is using the icing to write out anything that makes you feel overwhelmed, anything that makes you cry on your pillow in silence every night before you fall asleep, anything you can't get off your chest, any pain that's stuck in the corner of your stomach, or any lingering thoughts that won't leave you in peace. Through the process of baking cookies, decorating them with your emotions, and finally eating them, you are transforming a sad feeling, memory, or impulse into something positive.

Use this recipe whenever:

You feel an overwhelming need to commit self-destructive actions,

You feel that negative emotions are overwhelming you,

You have recurring negative or pessimistic thoughts, or . . .

You have the urge to eat cookies.

Makes about two dozen cookies, or 24 cookies, or however you wanna put it.

Ingredients:

- 2 sticks butter
- 1 cup sugar
- 1/8 cup powdered sugar
- 2 1/2 cups all-purpose flour

Instructions:

1. Preheat oven to 325 degrees.

2. Using a blender or a spatula, soften the butter until it has a smooth texture.

3. Once this is done, add half of the sugar and fold it in until fully incorporated.

4. Combine the rest of the sugar with the powdered sugar and add to the dough, along with the flour, until all the ingredients are thoroughly mixed.

5. Sprinkle some flour onto a clean, dry cutting board or on a Silpat (if you have one).

6. Roll out the dough until it is half a centimeter in thickness. You can measure it using the ruler you've had in your house since you were in the fifth grade.

7. Cut the dough with the mold of your choice. If you don't have a cookie cutter, use a knife to make figurines of whatever you like.

8. Place the dough on a sheet pan and bake for ten to fifteen minutes. Keep an eye on them so they don't begin to brown.

9. Allow cookies to cool on a rack.

Icing for decorating the cookies/writing your feelings on them

Ingredients:

- 1/2 cup powdered sugar
- 2 teaspoons milk
- Your choice of food coloring

Instructions:

1. Add the sugar and milk to a bowl and mix with a whisk or spoon.

2. Mix until the consistency is like toothpaste but a little bit softer. You can do this by adding a little bit more powdered sugar or a little bit less milk.

3. Add in the food coloring of your choice, put the mixture into a piping bag, and start writing. Some ideas for what to write:

IDEA # 2

WONDERING WHETHER
GETTING MY TEETH
WHITENED WILL HELP
ME FIND LOVE AGAIN

IDEA # 3

IDEA # 4

IDEA # 5

WANTING TO STICK A
WAD OF GUM IN THE
NEW BOYFRIEND'S /
GIRLFRIEND'S HAIR

IDEA # 6

Eggs and Rice

(A vegetarian option.)

This is a new take on a Colombian classic, and also serves as a way to measure your emotional state.

ABLE TO COOK EGGS AND RICE: GOOD

UNABLE TO COOK EGGS AND RICE: BAD

Serves 1 (for someone who is really hungry because heartbreak has taken away any sense of proportion or decent food portions. If this is not the case, you can share with your friend and/or dog).

Regular ingredients:

- 1/8 white onion, finely chopped
- 1 clove finely minced garlic
- 1/2 tablespoon olive oil
- 2 cups water
- 1/8 bell pepper, diced
- 1/4 scallion or green onion
- 1 teaspoon salt
- 2 cups white rice
- 3 eggs
- 1 tablespoon butter
- Salt to taste

Magical ingredients:

(Necessary for making hogao, a Colombian otherworldly sauce that is used as a base for typical dishes or as a topping for basically anything from arepas to yuca frita. *Hogao* comes from the word *ahogado*, which literally translates "to drown." And that is no coincidence—we know you are drowning in your own despair and sorrow, and we think this recipe can help. Kind of.)

- 1 teaspoon vegetable oil
- 1 1/2 scallions, finely chopped
- 1 clove garlic, minced
- 2 fresh tomatoes, diced
- 4 tablespoons water
- Salt to taste

Instructions for the magical ingredients for the hogao:

1. Sauté the scallions and garlic in a saucepan with the vegetable oil.

2. Add salt.

3. Add the rest of the ingredients and cook, stirring constantly until the liquid reduces.

4. Adjust the seasoning as you prefer.

5. Save for later.

Instructions for the first part of the recipe:

Makes about 4 cups cooked rice

1. Sauté the onion and garlic in a saucepan with the olive oil. (For a truly Colombian result, avoid the usual rice cooker and go for a pot or, as we would call it in my home, a caldero.)

2. Add the water, bell pepper, scallion, and half teaspoon salt.

3. Add rice and bring to a boil.

4. Reduce heat, cover, and simmer for fifteen minutes.

5. Once the rice has absorbed all the water, remove from heat and set aside.

Note: If you are feeling super lazy, you can just use leftover rice that is sitting in your fridge. Silvana says it could actually make this recipe taste better.

6. Beat 2 eggs in a bowl and add half a teaspoon of salt.

7. Melt the butter in a pan and add the beaten eggs and 1 cup of the cooked rice.

8. Stir until everything is combined and the eggs are fully cooked but moist.

9. Fry the other egg in a saucepan with some butter.

10. Serve the rice and top it with the fried egg and some hogao.

Chocolate Chip Cookies

While technically known as chocolate chip cookies, these should really be called "cookies for getting over despair." If these don't cheer you up, I don't know what will.

Makes about two dozen.

Ingredients:

- 1 1/2 cup sugar
- 1 cup melted butter
- 1 egg
- 1/2 tablespoon vanilla
- 1 1/2 cup wheat flour
- 1 pinch baking soda
- 1/4 teaspoon baking powder
- 1/2 teaspoon salt
- 8 ounces semisweet chocolate chips (at least 53 percent cacao)

Instructions:

1. Mix the butter and sugar until fluffy.

2. Combine the egg with the vanilla and add it to the butter mixture.

3. In a bowl, combine the flour, salt, baking soda, and baking powder, then add to the mixture. Mix everything together.

4. Add chocolate chips and mix them in.

5. Divide into portions using an ice cream scoop, depending on how many cookies you'd like. Put them on parchment paper, separated enough so they don't stick together.

6. Freeze for 15 to 30 minutes.

7. Bake at 350 degrees F for approximately twelve minutes.

In severe cases of despair, immediately convert the cookies into an ice cream sandwich.

Instructions:

1. Grab a scoop of your favorite ice cream.

2. Place the ice cream between two cookies.

3. Devour.

Pancakes in a Caserola

A classic recipe that can be modified depending on your state of mind or level of anger. If you feel like adding fruit, for example, your heart is telling you something very different than if you feel like adding whipped cream, dulce de leche, ice cream, or all three.

The heart oftentimes speaks through cravings.

5 servings

Ingredients:

- 1 cup wheat flour
- 2 tablespoons sugar
- 1/2 teaspoon baking powder
- 1/2 teaspoon salt
- 1 cup milk
- 1 egg
- 2 tablespoons melted butter
- 1 tablespoon oil or butter

Instructions:

Okay, so here is the part where I explain what a caserola is and no, it's not a casserole. A caserola is a small pan that comes with a lid and is mainly used to prepare fried eggs but can be used for cooking whatever you feel like cooking. Most Colombians make their pancakes in this tiny kitchen appliance, which is the secret to their extra fluffiness. Of course you can make your pancakes any way you like best, but since you are sad and depressed, we thought a new culinary adventure could suit you. Or not. It's your choice.

1. Mix the flour, sugar, baking powder, and salt in a bowl.

2. Add the milk and egg and whisk to prevent lumps from forming.

3. Add 2 tablespoons melted butter to the mixture.

4. Add the oil or more butter to a pan or caserola over low heat, followed by the pancake batter.

5. Cover so it cooks faster.

6. Cook until the pancakes begin to bubble and are firm enough to flip with a spatula.

7. Garnish with bananas, blueberries, strawberries, whipped cream, ice cream, or whatever your heart desires, and serve.

Croissant Bread Pudding

This recipe can either go really well or really badly.

Let the result be a measure of your emotional progress.

4 to 6 servings

Ingredients:

- 2 teaspoons granulated sugar
- 3 croissants
- 1 egg
- 2 tablespoons sugar
- 2/3 cup milk
- 1/2 cup heavy cream
- 1/2 teaspoon vanilla
- 1 1/2 teaspoon brandy
- 2 tablespoons raisins (optional)
- 1 tablespoon butter
- Powdered sugar for sprinkling
- Ice cream (optional)

Instructions:

1. Preheat oven to 350 degrees F.

2. Grease a small ramekin with butter and then cover with granulated sugar.

3. Cut the croissant into small, equally sized pieces (about half an inch) and place in a bowl.

4. Whisk the egg in a small bowl.

5. In a small saucepan, mix the milk, cream, and sugar.

6. Bring the pot to a boil and immediately pour the hot mixture over the eggs, whisking constantly.

7. Immediately return the mixture to the pot and bring it back to a boil, stirring it with a spatula.

8. Remove from heat and add the vanilla and brandy.

9. Pour the mixture over the croissant pieces and add raisins (if you are using raisins).

10. Mix thoroughly until the bread has absorbed all the liquid.

11. Spoon equal portions into ramekins without pressing too hard.

12. Bake for ten to twelve minutes or until the bread begins to brown.

13. Sprinkle with powdered sugar.

14. Serve hot or cold with a scoop of ice cream.

No-Bake Cheesecake

Perfect if you forgot to pay your gas or electric bill because you've been crying in bed for so long.

6 servings

For the cheesecake:

Ingredients:

- 1/4 cup sugar
- 1 cup cream cheese
- 1/4 teaspoon lemon juice
- 1/2 teaspoon orange juice
- 1/2 teaspoon vanilla
- 1/2 cup heavy cream

Instructions:

1. Using a mixer, combine half of the sugar with the cream cheese.

2. Mix in the lemon juice, orange juice, and vanilla.

3. In a separate bowl, mix the heavy cream with the remaining sugar until the whipped cream is firm.

4. Using a spatula, combine the whipped cream with the cream cheese mixture, folding in. The idea is for it to be somewhat spongy.

5. Put it in a piping bag and refrigerate for an hour.

For the cookie crumble:

Ingredients:

- 4 shortbread cookies
- 1/4 cup butter
- 2 tablespoons sugar
- strawberries, blueberries, and/ or raspberries (as many as you like)
- 1 squeeze of lemon juice

Instructions:

1. Preheat oven to 325 degrees F.

2. Put the cookies in a plastic bag and finely crush them using a rolling pin.

3. Melt the butter in a pan.

4. Mix in the crushed cookies and sugar.

5. Place the mixture in a baking tin or on parchment paper and bake for five minutes or until the cookie has browned.

6. Remove from the oven and allow to cool.

To serve:

1. Slice some of the strawberries, blueberries, and/or raspberries and add some lemon juice.

2. Spoon some of the cream cheese mixture (also known as our no-bake cheesecake) into a clear glass.

3. Add berry slices and sprinkle with cookie crumbs.

4. Continue alternating the cream cheese mixture with the berries and cookie crumbles to create layers.

5. Serve cold or refrigerate to enjoy later.

Grilled Cheese Sandwich with Fries

Professional chefs will use a pan instead of a sandwich maker or a panini press just as there are spiritual teachers who don't need this book. It's their loss.

1 serving

For the grilled cheese sandwich:

Ingredients:

- 2 loaves of brioche, sourdough, or pain de mie
- Butter to taste
- 4 thin slices of Gruyère cheese
- 2 slices of Gouda cheese
- 2 tablespoons red onion marmalade (instructions below)

Instructions:

1. Slice the bread and spread one piece with the red onion marmalade.

2. Butter the outer part of both slices.

3. Add the cheeses between the slices, and place the sandwich in the sandwich maker.

To serve:

1. Cut diagonally into triangles.

2. Serve on a nice plate. After all, it's for you.

3. Add a side of fries (you can either make them at home or buy them anywhere).

For the red onion marmalade:

Ingredients:

- 1/2 red onion
- 1/2 tablespoon olive oil
- 1/4 teaspoon salt
- 1/2 tablespoon sugar
- 1/2 teaspoon balsamic vinegar
- Orange zest (optional)

Instructions:

1. Dice the onion and sauté in olive oil over medium heat until it becomes translucent.

2. Add salt.

3. Add sugar and cook for another five minutes or until the onion is soft.

4. Add the balsamic vinegar and orange zest.

5. Remove from heat and allow to cool.

Oven Roasted Chicken

This is a good recipe because for a couple of hours it will keep you occupied with something other than your own sadness. If you follow the instructions to a T, you'll come out feeling like a little chef yourself and therefore able to conquer anything.

4 servings

Ingredients:

- 1 whole chicken
- 2 cloves garlic, finely minced
- 2 tablespoons butter
- 6 sprigs of thyme
- 6 small carrots, peeled and cut in half
- 1 leek (the white part only) cut in half
- 1 white onion cut in quarters
- 5 small red russet potatoes
- 2 tablespoons olive oil
- 2 teaspoons salt
- 1 teaspoon pepper

Instructions:

1. Preheat oven to 450 degrees F.

2. Pat the chicken dry with a paper towel to get rid of any moisture.

3. Combine the minced garlic with a pinch of salt, and coat the chicken inside and out.

4. Play with the butter as you would with some PlayDoh (make sure your hands are clean). Once the butter is soft, coat the chicken inside out with it. Playing with the butter will help you loosen up.

5. Season the inside of the chicken with salt and pepper. Add six sprigs of thyme.

6. Place the chicken on a baking sheet breasts up and tie up the wings and legs.

7. Peel and slice the carrots in halves. Cut the leek in half lengthwise.

8. Slice the white onion into four equal pieces.

9. Mix the potatoes with the other vegetables, season with salt, pepper, thyme, and olive oil. Place the vegetables on the baking sheet around the chicken, season with salt, and sprinkle with a little more olive oil.

10. Bake for twenty-five minutes.

11. Reduce the temperature to 400 degrees F and continue to bake for another thirty to forty minutes or until the internal temperature of the chicken thighs reads 165 degrees F.

13. Plate and serve.

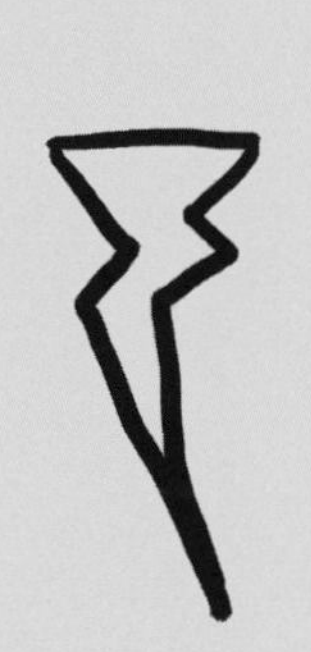

Acknowledgments

Thanks to everyone who helped me make this book a reality. And SPECIAL thanks to everyone who broke the hearts of those who helped me, because without them, this book wouldn't exist.

To Andrea Montejo, for not running for the hills when I told her I wanted world domination, for the undisputed support, for helping me make my dreams come true, and for giving birth to my favorite person on earth: YES, JULIÁN, I AM TALKING ABOUT YOU. YOU ROCK.

To Meg Leder for being the smartest, kindest, coolest, and most talented editor in the world. (You know you have found your match when your editor delivers brilliant editorial direction and up-to-date celebrity gossip in the same email.) Your belief in this book and, more important, your friendship and guidance throughout this process have meant the world to me.

To Shannon Kelly, thank you for taking care of every little detail, for making sure everything runs smoothly, and for making me feel less alone in the world of people who REALLY love cleaning and organizing stuff. I admire you.

To Chris Dufault, for actually thinking that pitching me as the Sofia Vergara of books is a good commercial strategy. Thank you for your friendship and good luck on your vegan journey.

To Patrick Nolan:

To Kate Stark, for the support, the fancy pizza, and for seeing my "The Thinker" tattoo for what it really means.

To everyone else at Penguin Books: Kathryn Court, Brianna Linden, Allison Carney, Sabila Khan, Sabrina Bowers, Brianna Harden, Fabiana Van Arsdell, Lindsay Prevette, John Lawton, Jenn

Lipman, and Lavina Lee, thank you for taking a chance on this girl from Cali, Colombia, and for being the best team an author can ask for.

To Ezra Fitz, thank you for making me sound good (and funny!) in English.

To Mom, who has fought so many battles with dignity, and who has taught me to be strong. To Santiago, for inspiring me more than you realize. To Dad, for making me happy at the time and for buying me all the books and markers a ten-year-old could have ever wanted (without them, none of this would have ever happened).

To Alejandro Gómez Dugand, Gloria Susana Esquivel, and Alejandra Algorta, for sitting down to edit, color, organize, and otherwise plan out this book with me. For making me feel like a millionaire at the Bank of Good Friends.

To Silvana Villegas, for bringing her talents to this book, for being my friend and family, for not judging me when I ask her the same exact thing every time we go out for a bite. To Julián Jaramillo and Oliver Siegenthaler, for inspiring me and believing in me.

To all the friends I abandoned when I locked myself away to work, and who will soon be receiving a copy of this book along with a letter asking for forgiveness. Are we still friends?

☐ Yes.

☐ No.

☐ Stop being so dramatic, Amalia.

To all those who read me online and always have something nice to say even though you don't know me. In real life, each and every one of your messages has moved me to tears.

To La Mamma, for giving me everything, for convincing me that I was destined for big things.

About the Author

© Faber Franco

Hi! I'm Amalia Andrade. I was born in Cali, Colombia, in 1986. I studied literature at Pontifical Xavierian University in Bogotá. I've been drawing forever. I've written for several magazines in both Colombia and the United States. I believe strongly in the power of keeping a diary. When I grow up I want to be a mix of Sylvia Plath and Tina Fey. I don't know what else to write, since my editor is making me do this and we all know that writing about yourself is impossible. I live in Bogotá with my cats.

WEB

www.amaliaandrade.com

FACEBOOK

Amalia Andrade

TWITTER

@amaliaandrade_

INSTAGRAM

amaliaandrade_

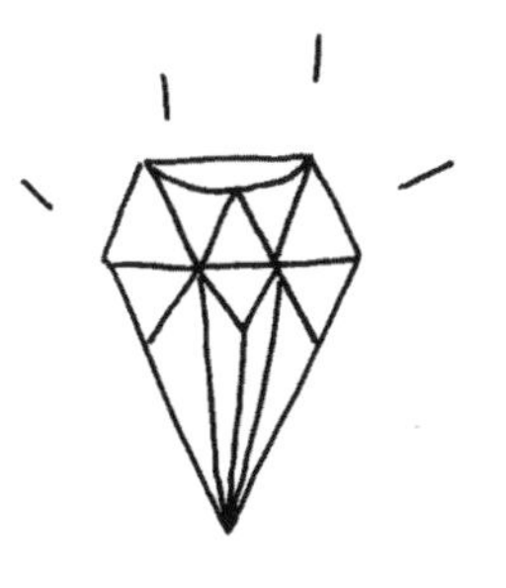